the

SECRET LANGUAGE

of Babies

the SECRET LANGUAGE of Babies

THE BODY LANGUAGE OF LITTLE BODIES

Sally & Edwin Kiester

FALL RIVER PRESS

Fall River Press
122 Fifth Avenue
New York, NY 10011

ISBN: 978-1-4351-1775-4

Printed and bound in China

3 5 7 9 10 8 6 4 2

Design: Ali Walper

NOTE

CONTENTS

INTRODUCTION

abies communicate from the moment they are born. Some would say they send messages earlier, during quickening, when the expectant mother first feels baby's kicks in her womb. Of course, these pre- or post-natal despatches are not composed of words found in the dictionary. Your baby learns at a very early age to use body movements as a means of communication. This body language is used to express emotions; to indicate what he or she likes or wants; to respond yes or no; to report that he or she is tired, wet, hungry, or cold; in short, to convey what's going on in his or her little head. Indeed, your baby, without uttering a single word, is able to tell you what he or she wants you to do and what results are expected. Speaking without words is the secret language of babies.

You may have already witnessed this sort of nonverbal communication at your own breakfast table. Eight-month-old Josh or Olivia is sitting in a high chair and has just polished off the morning juice. Your infant holds out the empty cup and emits a fervent *"uh-uh-uh."* The staccato syllables don't mean much, but the gesture certainly does, and

only the most preoccupied parent could miss the message: *"More juice! More juice!"* Not all of Baby's messages will be this simple to read, however, and examining an infant's many and varied means of communication can help you interpret this "secret language" consistently and accurately—ensuring both a contented baby and confident parent.

GETTING THE MESSAGE ACROSS

By thrusting the juice cup at you, Josh or Olivia is demonstrating a budding understanding of the human communication process. Baby makes a statement, often an emphatic demand, and he or she expects you to respond and take some action to satisfy the demand. The demand, of course, is not stated in words but in movements, gestures, or body language, and is often accompanied by gurgles or wails. No matter. It is the beginning of the kind of request-response-action dialogue that your child will eventually and effortlessly use dozens of times each day in his or her life. Already, Baby Josh, despite his tender age, fully understands that communication is two-way: *"I send the adults a message, they receive it, and then they do (or don't do) what I want them to do. I can generate their actions."*

THE FOUNDING FATHER

Much of what we know about the secret language of babies and how they think, learn, and communicate rests on the teachings of Jean Piaget (1896–1980). Although some of his ideas have since been modified or reversed by more recent research, this Swiss biologist-psychologist is still regarded as the father of child development and its most influential figure. Until Piaget, scientists, led by Sigmund Freud, sought to understand children by looking at them backward, as adults. Piaget turned the equation around, studying their early development to discern how they progressed into adulthood.

A father himself, Piaget began by carefully observing and recording the behavior of his own three children from birth to eighteen months. He recognized that children were not simply little adults or adults-in-training, but thought and behaved differently from grown-ups. As a biologist he explained some of this development in terms of physical growth, including changes in the brain itself. But he also described child development in psychological, social, and emotional terms.

Piaget described a child's development in four stages and substages, leading to full-fledged maturation around age fifteen. It is this "stage" theory that has been most questioned. Piaget believed children started life virtually at ground zero. He believed, for instance, that until about age seven months, children's senses were independent. They could not connect what they saw with what they touched or heard. Scientists have now shown that babies can unify input from different senses within the first few hours of life. Furthermore, Piaget believed that babies were not able to imitate adults' expressions until they were four months old. It is now known that they can reproduce facial expressions as early as the first forty-two minutes of life.

Despite the advances made since his time, Piaget's ideas remain the foundation of child development study and of early childhood education, particularly with his theory that children learn through play.

Although Miss Manners may not approve of gesturing with an outstretched index finger, the fact is that pointing is a basic gesture of communication regularly used by children and adults alike—and it is a vital means of communication, particularly for Baby. An alert nine-month-old is curious and exploratory, seeking to understand the mysterious world, but is not yet mobile enough to conduct explorations on his or her own. Most of the things Josh or Olivia is curious about and wants to touch, feel, rub, taste, squeeze, or cuddle are frustratingly beyond reach. The only way to get close to those fascinating objects is to extend a chubby forefinger in their direction, attract Mom's attention with movements or noises, and wait expectantly for her to understand. *"You want the lorry? No. You want the rattle? No. Oh, the teddy. Of course, the teddy. Here, sweetheart. Here's your teddy."* Mission accomplished. And pointing will express other messages as well, as Baby matures and develops more sophisticated needs.

That babies can express themselves before they can form words is part of a new and exciting understanding of infant development. Before the 1970s the experts held that babies couldn't communicate or even think in the adult definition of the term until they could use nouns and verbs like the rest of us. When babies moved in a certain way or seemed to smile, it was believed to be merely a conditioned response or a reflex like an infant's instinctive sucking. Parents' hands-on experience with baby and their common sense seemed to tell them otherwise, but they often didn't trust their own observations. *"I swear he smiled at me,"* a mother would say of her three-week-old, *"but I know that can't be true."*

Baby Olivia, we were once advised, was a *tabula rasa*, a clean slate on which her parents, her environment, and society could fill in the details of her personality and character. Baby Olivia herself was a know-nothing in the literal sense. Why, she couldn't even get her act together! Before the age of four months, she was unable to make connections between even her own basic senses; touch, smell, hearing, vision, and taste all worked independently, parents were told. When Baby was picked up and held close and soothing songs were whispered to her, she didn't realize that the warm cuddling hands, the loving face peering down at her, and the melodic "tra's" and "la's" all were part of the same person. They could have come from three different directions. In fact, according to the developmental science of the time, Olivia, at that early age, didn't even know that she was a person. Even her chubby baby hands, crossing her line of sight, registered only as a couple of unidentified flying objects. They could have belonged to anything or anybody.

That view of infancy—once widely accepted and now rejected by most experts—greatly underestimated babies, according to Andrew Meltzoff, of the University of Washington. Meltzoff, one of a growing body of international scientists whose research has overturned the previous school of thought, coauthored *The Scientist in the Crib*, along with Alison Gopnik and Patricia Kuhl. In this ground-breaking work he explains that babies are thinking, inquisitive creatures from the moment they are born, and they immediately set out to discover where they fit into the "blooming, buzzing confusion," as philosopher William James calls the newborn's world. They are indeed aware of their surroundings and instinctively know much more about themselves than they had previously been given credit for. Infants can sense how their bodies work, and they demonstrate that by turning their heads to locate a sudden sound. Far from a tabula rasa for us to shape and mold, babies write on their own slates and even guide our hands as we attempt to add our own inscriptions. And although your children are no longer considered "blank slates" to be filled in, you should not feel that your responsibilities have been diminished. Rather, Meltzoff's discoveries encourage today's parents to be as attentive as possible from the outset of life—even a newborn baby, we now know, will make some attempt to communicate to you and through you to understand his or her world.

Our new and improved understanding of infant development draws from many sources—biology, for one. Human babies are helpless longer and take longer to mature than any of our fellow primates. But, in other respects, they are remarkably similar. They show the same mother-child attachment as monkeys—and geese, too. Their brains develop in a fashion similar to that of chimpanzees and other great apes, although here, too, humans develop at a more gradual pace and take more time to mature.

Anthropology also teaches us something about the development of babies. It has been observed that across the world's many and varied cultures, babies all develop particular behaviors and reach developmental milestones at the same pace. They sit up, babble, point at interesting objects, and say their first words on the same timetable, whether in the Amazon, the Himalayas, Spain, or Saratoga.

ACCENTS ARE FOREVER

Although babies can't talk at six months, by that time they are already good listeners. They take in and file for future use the nuances of language—the pronunciations and mispronunciations they hear at cribside. And when words do come, they will be spoken with the distinctive, localized twang or lilt overheard in Mom's and Dad's speech. Accents form early, in whatever language, and stubbornly hang on for a lifetime.

Patricia Kuhl of the University of Washington established that accents form early in an ingenious experiment with American and Japanese children. Japanese adults tend to struggle with the "L" and "R" sounds common in English. Kuhl's experiment showed that six-month-olds in Tokyo perceive that "L" and "R" are different sounds just as easily as American six-month-olds do. But by one year they couldn't distinguish between the two.

Kuhl used a head-turn technique to make her discovery. In Kuhl's lab, a mother sat with her baby in her lap, facing an experimenter who held a toy to keep the baby's attention. A loudspeaker chanted "La-la-la" at one-second intervals while the baby watched the toy and listened. Then the speaker changed to "La-la-ra." Immediately, a plastic box lit up and a teddy bear began to beat on a toy drum. The baby turned to watch. A video camera recorded the turns.

At the age of six months, two of three Japanese and American kids turned to watch, cued by the speaker's change. At age one year, 80 percent of Americans turned, but only 59 percent of Japanese turned, little better than chance. To them, the two sounds had become the same. In another example of neurological maturation, the nerve pathways that were no longer used had been pruned away, and those that were used and reinforced had developed and strengthened.

In the new view of infant development, the crucial way in which Josh and Olivia resemble the offspring of other species is that they recognize early that they are surrounded by others "like me." That lightbulb going off inspires the urge to communicate with those "like me." This recognition is the foundation of babies' secret language and oral communication as well. Josh and Olivia recognize that the smiling mom and the doting dad bending over the crib are "like me." They instinctively know at some primordial level that, because they are helpless, it is in their best interest to recognize and reach out to those who will feed, cleanse, and protect them; thus the "like me" link is forged. This recognition of interconnectedness is more than a survival instinct, though. It is also the start of social behavior, the intertwining of the newcomer's existence into the social fabric. Josh and Olivia are now

social animals, and must connect their lives with those of other social animals—thus, the need to communicate, by whatever means available.

Scientific spirit apart, perhaps what has contributed most to the new child development paradigm are the advances in technology. The video camera, coupled with the ingenuity of science, has opened a window on infant behavior only dimly suspected before. By using surveillance cameras like those in your local convenience store and videotaping each twitch of the arms and legs, every smile and frown, and all nuances of behavior, scientists are now able to study all the subtleties that previous experts—and even the most vigilant of parents—had missed. Sensitive lenses, for example, zero in on little eyes and not only keep track of where the eyes are focused but also ingeniously record the images that the baby is seeing and the amount of time it takes for these images to capture and hold the baby's visual attention. Tiny recording devices attached to crib mattresses pick up every sound, both of movement and vocalization, and these recordings can be correlated with the videotaped observations.

Moreover, scientists began to use technology to set up sophisticated test events to watch babies reactions to a variety of situations. For example, in one study, videotaped pictures of Mom's face side by side with that of another woman were shown to Baby to determine which face he preferred. Not surprisingly, the image-capturing lenses confirmed that Mom was always the favorite. Going one step further, the researchers projected faces of Mom smiling and Mom frowning and observed the baby's facial expression change accordingly.

Meanwhile, neurobiologists and neuroanatomists learned more about how the baby's brain developed. Basically, they learned that an infant is born with billions of interconnected brain cells and that, as the brain develops, the neural connections used frequently are strengthened, and those not used are discarded. Thus the baby's burgeoning brain allows him to reach and grasp, to focus unerringly on Mom's face, and to observe, store away, and remember patterns of useful and acceptable behavior for retrieval and reproduction later. Each time a behavior is repeated, the neural circuitry is reinforced. Movements and reactions that bring no results or response are discarded.

From all these discoveries and advancements grew a different picture of baby communication. The waggles and wriggles of newborns, we now know, are not random but—even from the earliest days of life—are a coordinated form of expression and a way of connecting with those around them. Still months away from putting messages into words, a baby will use body movements—increasingly punctuated with coos and gurgles—to express his needs, his wants, and even his emotions. The all-seeing video camera, for instance, showed that even when Mom's shadow inadvertently fell across the crib, the six-week-old reacted with an excited and predictable pattern of wriggling and arm windmilling. And when Mom spoke in the soothing tones of mothers everywhere, Baby's movements were keyed to the rhythm of her voice. And, more importantly, the studies showed that whenever Mom responded to Baby's body language in a way that communicated "message received," that means of communication was reinforced and hardwired into the baby's brain.

SAY CHEESE

THE SIGNIFICANCE OF THE FIRST SMILE

WHAT BABY DOES

Smiles shyly and makes eye contact.

WHAT BABY MEANS

"I like to look at your face."

WHAT YOU SHOULD NOTICE

Baby is already trying to connect with you.

People will tell you that your baby's first fetching smile isn't real. Little overfed Daniel is just passing gas. He's opening his lips wide to get rid of some of that carbon dioxide that's distending his insides. That "smile," you will be told, is just a burp in disguise. You'd like to think it's a smile, but it isn't.

Well, don't believe it. Your baby, like all babies, likes to look at faces more than anything else. Once Daniel can control the focus of his eyes and turn his head toward the face peering down into his crib, he fixes his gaze on the human countenance. And he prefers his mother's face first and foremost. And she smiles. Experiment after experiment demonstrates that, shown a picture of Mom and a picture of an unknown woman, a baby will unerringly fix on Mom and keep his eyes there. He will flash a widening, gummy grin and gaze directly into her eyes. Daniel isn't gassy; he's saying, "Mom, I like looking at you!" Your baby is a natural flirt, and who could resist his flirtation?

His body language is reinforced by your actions—your delighted smile in response and your bending down to touch him nose to nose. He loves that attention. He begins to make the association: If I do this thing with my mouth and eyes, Mom will do something with her mouth and eyes too, and she'll touch me. I like that.

Smiles have been seen as early as a few hours after birth—fleeting smiles, with a modest upturn at the margins of the mouth. Those tiny, off-and-on smiles continue over the next several weeks. Sometime around three or four weeks, there's an unmistakable smile, with bright eyes and the whole face lighting up. Mom is hooked, and she and Baby are hereafter linked together. There is, of course, a biological explanation for this phenomenon. It's essential for Baby, helpless and needy as he is, to forge a strong emotional link with the person who will protect him and take care of him. Thus monkeys cling to their mothers and goslings trail after theirs.

BEHIND THE SIGNS

Baby's First Conversations

Babies actually "converse" with their grown-up caregivers. See for yourself. Bend down toward your baby and say, "Pretty baby! Aren't you a pretty baby?" or just make cooing, affectionate sounds and smile. Little Jennifer is likely to make her own cooing sounds, windmill her tiny arms and legs, and smile—in gleeful recognition of the attention. You grin and say more soft words; she responds with gurgles, kicks, and waves, often in the same rhythm. You talk; she waits and then "answers" just like grown-ups do. Child-development experts call these exchanges "proto-conversations." They are an important step toward actual speech; the baby learns that communication is a two-way process.

MOM, YOU'RE THE ONE

If a mother bends over her baby's crib along with another woman, she will notice how Baby's eyes go to her and stay there. Maybe a quick flick of curiosity about the other, but she's the one Baby likes to look at. It's Mom first and always, the target of the early smile.

Daniel's first genuine "social smile" also marks an important first step in his emotional development. That initial toothless grin clearly says, "Hello world! Hello Mom! I'm here and I see you." It's the beginning of intersubjectivity, the recognition that persons close to him are familiar and are bound to him. Baby's smile at this stage also means "Hey! You're a lot like me. I understand that you make up part of my world." It's a way of identifying himself with the human race. He now clearly recognizes that there is a world beyond himself. He looks out between the bars of the crib and sees things and people that cross his line of vision and touch his existence, usually for the better. These people and objects affect his well-being, and thus he has feelings about them, mirrored in the crinkling of his tiny face. Until now his life has been centered on individual physical need; he has been a more or less passive creature to be fed, diapered, bathed, cuddled, and kept warm. Now Daniel is reaching out to others. His new and improved smile sends a message. It is the beginning of communication.

BEHIND THE SIGNS

The Value of a Smile

The importance of a smile can be observed in the way a baby reacts to her mother's face. For example, if the mother's face is impassive and unemotional, or if she is showing signs of sadness, Baby won't like that at all. Her own face will show her unhappiness. She'll ball up her fists, kick the sides of the crib or high chair, avert her eyes, and wave her arms to try to generate a reaction. Picking her up and smiling to show that Mom is happy will help smooth the frown from Baby's face and may well produce a glowing smile in return.

Baby Fact

Babies can produce real smiles as early as three days old—but most babies start smiling at three to four weeks old.

In the days and weeks ahead he will reach out more and more. He will develop and demonstrate other emotions—anger, frustration, joy, playfulness, puzzlement, and mischief—about what he sees and what is having an impact on his life.

The infant brain is complex, and no one can say precisely which parts link with the others or which route a given message takes from one part of the brain to another. The best theory is that the "thinking" part (the cortex in the forebrain) takes in information and distributes it elsewhere for action and reaction. One immediate and important target is the amygdala, considered to be the seat of emotion. Simplified, Baby sees Mom and the cortex asks the amygdala, "How do I feel about her?" The amygdala tells the cortex, "I like her!" The cortex tells the facial muscles, "Smile." And they do.

BEHIND THE SIGNS

Why Doesn't He Smile at Grandma?

You know the scene: Grandma comes to visit her young grandson. She smiles delightedly, even kootchykoos him with her finger. And to her dismay, he wriggles away, turns his head, and maybe even bursts into tears.

Babies learn early that smiles are meant for certain special people. They're not to be bestowed on everyone, just the familiar faces that care for them and those with whom there's a special bond and attachment. This kind of selectivity is particularly prominent in the latter half of the first year of life, coinciding with the common phenomenon of "stranger anxiety," when Baby feels threatened and shrinks from unfamiliar faces.

All these connections are in place when a baby is born. But the brain is a work in progress. As it develops and a baby's world opens, the connections not used are shorn away and those used repeatedly—as Mom adoringly bends over the crib—grow stronger and stronger. Each time Baby smiles and Mom smiles back, the connection is strengthened. Although this response is natural (what mother could resist returning her baby's smile?) it is also developmentally crucial in order to strengthen that brain pathway. A smiling baby who does not receive a smile in return will soon stop smiling. A famous scientific study examined children in an Eastern European orphanage who had received tragically little emotional input. At six months old, they still were unable to respond to a smile.

Baby Fact

Call a five-month-old by name, and she will turn to look at you.

THE SMILING TIMETABLE

Babies' smiles are a work in progress. Studying many hours of videotape, Colwyn Trevarthen at the University of Edinburgh, Scotland, has detected baby smiles as early as three days after birth. But these occur fleetingly at the corners of the mouth. From there, smiles progress:

3–4 WEEKS	The corners of the mouth really turn up and the eyes brighten and look directly at you.
3 MONTHS	The smile widens. The mouth opens, the whole face lights up, and dimples appear in the cheeks in a genuinely happy smile.
5–6 MONTHS	A real, gleeful, happy smile with an open mouth and tongue showing. The expression seems to say, "I'm delighted!"
7–8 MONTHS	Baby laughs aloud and grins happily at your smiling face.

WINDOWS TO THE SOUL

CONNECTING TO YOUR NEWBORN THROUGH EYE CONTACT

WHAT BABY DOES
Stares directly into your eyes.

WHAT BABY MEANS
"Please take care of me."

WHAT YOU SHOULD NOTICE
Baby understands that you are "like her"
and that you will care for her.

ittle Mei is brought to you for friendship and feeding shortly after birth. She's quiet and wide awake, not fussing or crying, and you hold her up to admire. Only inches away from her nose, you realize she's looking right into your eyes as you're looking into hers. Your gazes lock. Yes, she's definitely making contact. Maybe she's not sending an explicit message, but nonetheless she's connecting with you and decidedly interested in what she sees. It's a thrilling moment for both of you.

That eye-to-eye electricity is Baby's first flash of communication, and the eyes will be a vital communication tool hereafter. The moment you look into her eyes and she returns the gaze introduces what the renowned researcher Colwyn Trevarthen of the University of Edinburgh has defined as "intersubjectivity." This term refers to the recognition that the two "subjects" early on become interlaced, sharing a common interest: their relationship. Newborn Mei discovers that she is not alone in this new and unfamiliar environment. There are other beings out there who appear very much like her but larger. They focus on her while she focuses on them. Intersubjectivity binds them together now and for the future. And on some basic level Mei understands that the person behind those close-up eyes will attend to her welfare, her wants and her needs, and her quest for companionship. Her eye contact sends a signal that she is ready to engage and connect with you. That first eye contact will last only a few seconds, but it will become longer and more frequent as the days pass.

She's a Head Turner!

One of the initial tests in a newborn's evaluation is to check his reactions to an individual sound. Early on she also turns to the sound of her mother's voice. This localization of sound soon extends to other sounds and voices. It was once held that localization comes much later. However, technology has advanced so far that coordinated sound and head-turning has been detected at a very early age.

The pioneering psychologist William James once described the newborn's world as one of "blooming, buzzing confusion." Science now agrees that it is much more organized than that.

There is another developmental landmark evident here. Mei can now direct her vision toward objects and people close to her that catch her interest: your face, the mobile hanging above her crib, the interesting images she sees through the crib bars. It used to be believed that newborns' eyes were not yet able to "track"—that is, they could not follow a moving object as it crossed their line of vision. The still developing tiny eye muscles presumably did not yet allow for that kind of movement. Today, those ubiquitous video cameras have shown us that Mei's eyes are indeed able to look at things, and she finds plenty to look at, right from the start.

A newborn sleeps sixteen to twenty hours out of twenty-four and is drowsy or half awake a few hours more. Only three to four hours are spent in the "quiet alert" phase. But during those minutes Mei is most aware of her surroundings, most responsive to those around her and most receptive to their overtures. She looks at objects, people, the brightly colored wallpaper. If you walk toward her, her eyes will widen as your shadow falls across her crib. Watch her and see her eyes shift as she takes in the novel environment. See her head turn to the side to take in a sight a few feet away.

Mei already has preferences for what she likes to look at. She chooses bright colors and bold patterns. Red zigzags are good; lavender circles are boring. This is why the best crib mobiles feature eye-catching reds and oranges and electric blues. Mei also likes to see movement. Even the flickering images on a television screen will catch her attention, although there is little evidence that she understands what she sees.

THE QUIET REVOLUTIONARY

Colwyn Trevarthen is a professor of psychology and psychobiology who looks like anything but a rebel. Yet with his observations on intersubjectivity between newborns and their caregivers, he dramatically overturned the accepted theories about newborns and their emotional development. Trevarthen said the link was grounded in human biology and was present from birth, similar to the attachment between mothers and offspring in other mammals. Previous scientists had had a psychoanalytic explanation, based on the teachings of Freud and the notion that the baby was a *tabula rasa*, a clean slate whose emotional attachments were shaped in the early years of life by the role of the mother. Trevarthen's 1950s ideas were disparaged at first but now have become accepted in the child-development field. Trevarthen has gone on to produce other landmark studies in children's emotional development. He has insisted that understanding a child's emotional development must be on an equal footing with understanding his physical growth. A particular interest for Trevarthen, himself a musician, has been the role of music in fostering a child's emotional development. He notes that rhythms are a factor in a child's life going back to the womb, where the mother's rhythmic breathing and heartbeat dominate his environment. In the twenty-first century, his research, not surprisingly, has focused on autistic children who often lack normal emotion.

Human faces, though, are Mei's absolute favorite thing to look at and to study. A little being who has seen her first face only hours before is surprisingly able to recognize a human countenance when she sees one. In one experiment, researchers projected above babies' cribs the distorted image of a human face. The mouth was where the forehead should be, and the eyes were placed together on one side of the face like a Cubist painting. Alongside this faux Picasso the experimenters projected a normal, smiling face. Babies focused on the normal face and gave the caricature only a fleeting glance.

Although great observers, newborn babies are extremely nearsighted. Mei focuses most sharply on objects only about 8 inches (21 cm) from her eyes. (Some specialists suggest the optimal distance may be closer to 15 inches [40 cm].) The focal length steadily increases with development. By three months, the baby can clearly see objects 6 feet (1.7 m) or more away.

Be aware of this. The lesson to you, the parent, is to hold your newborn up close—*en face*—and emphasize eye contact. It's also a good reason to suspend a bright mobile at a short distance from Baby in the crib, where she can focus on it and study it.

Holding a baby en face also maximizes hearing potential. Although normal newborns can certainly hear, they are sensitive at first to a limited range of sounds, roughly 200–500 hertz. That's the approximate range of a higher-register human voice. Parents worldwide indeed speak to their babies in this register, in the distinctive voice traditionally known as "motherese," and more recently dubbed "child-directed speech," or CDS.

to recognize the face so early? Several researchers theorize that recognition of fellow humans is an inborn quality that is essential to the survival of the species. That recognition of others "like me" is akin to that of newly hatched ducklings, who emerge from the shell able to identify mother and fellow ducklings and to cluster about them. Because the ducklings are vulnerable to predators, says Susan Goldin-Meadow of the University of Chicago, it is important for them to distinguish their kindred (who will protect them) from others (who might eat them). Human babies, who are even more helpless than ducklings in early life, have an inborn ability to know who will protect and nurture them. They instinctively gravitate to the "like me" types who will see to their welfare. "Here I am, Mom and Dad," those piercing eyes say. "I'm yours to love and care for."

In high treble, drawing out the syllables for greater comprehension, they say, "Helloooh, Baaaybee! Aren't you a prettee baaaybee?" Child-directed speech is some two octaves higher than a normal voice and is delivered in a sing-song manner and in rhythms and melody that catch the baby's attention. Researchers and their tape recorders have caught women speaking unmistakable "motherese" as far apart as Taiwan, Australia, Spain, and Turkey. Even fathers, the researchers found, lift their voices an octave from their normal tenors or baritones to a kind of alto when addressing newborns.

How is it that a baby who has never seen a human face before birth (and afterward perhaps only some masked faces in the delivery room) seems

Baby Fact

Even though a baby has poor distance vision, she is aware of distant objects that move. She will turn her head toward a moving car or a tree blowing in the wind.

MAGIC MOBILE

As Baby grows, he will quickly begin to learn about cause and effect. He will learn that actions can be taken that will produce results, and these results can be anticipated.

For example, if Mom were to tie one end of a bright red ribbon to a mobile and the other end to Baby's toe, she would see this process in action. When Baby wiggles his foot, the mobile will move, and in a short time he will realize that he is making the mobile move and he can do it voluntarily.

If the ribbon were untied, Baby would continue to wiggle his toes and become confused that the mobile remains still.

I SPY

BABY BEGINS TO VISUALLY CONNECT WITH THE WORLD

WHAT BABY DOES
Moves her eyes around trying to take everything in.

WHAT BABY MEANS
"Everything is so interesting!"

WHAT YOU SHOULD NOTICE
*Baby can now see her surroundings
and wants to learn more about them.*

One sunny afternoon you walk into the nursery to check on seven-week-old Josie or just to admire her sleeping form. To your surprise, Josie is wide awake and alert. She seems to be studying the wall above her crib, her eyes locked on the bright sunshine dancing and playing over her head. The eyes turn to look at your face; there's a flickering smile and the eyes move again. This time they focus on a balloon held by a teddy bear on the nursery wallpaper. It's a bright red balloon, and her gaze stays there.

Under two months of age, Josie and her contemporaries prefer to look at human faces. They especially like the familiar ones of Mother, Father, and siblings. But gradually, attention and visual skills broaden to include objects as well as people. Besides those humans looming over her crib, she likes to study the furniture in the nursery, the lamp, the toys, and anything bright and colorful. When she was a newborn, Josie couldn't see effectively more than a foot away, the distance between her parent's nose and her own when she was held *en face*. Now she can clearly take in anything within a 5- to 6-foot (1.5–1.8 m) range.

Of her major senses of taste, smell, hearing, touch, and sight, Josie's sight is the last to fully develop. Even when she is a newborn, you will see her react to a sweet taste on her lips or crinkle her nose at a disagreeable odor. A full year will pass before her vision could be called normal, matching the 20/20 vision of an adult. What she sees at a distance, meanwhile, is fuzzy, dim, and wavering. You project a sharper image when you lean over and hold her close than when you first appear in the doorway. Still, this improved vision at seven weeks furnishes her with a new tool with which to understand her world.

Pendulum Power

Now that you know your three-month-old can track with his eyes, you can have fun with him. With Baby lying on his back, dangle a scarf or ribbon above his eyes, about a foot away, not close enough for him to reach. Then slowly swing the scarf from side to side above his face like a pendulum. You'll see his eyes move in tandem with the tantalizing fabric. You'll probably also hear him squeal with delight. Don't overdo it, though. Watch for signs of boredom.

Some images penetrate this fog better than others. As their vision gets better, babies show a distinct preference for bright, striking colors, which is why Josie will zero in on the red balloon held by the bear and not the pale yellow one held by the bunny next to it. Bold patterns are more popular than more subtle ones (a circular bull's-eye gets more attention than a checkerboard) as researchers have discovered with their informative zoom lenses. When a circular pattern is projected next to a pattern of ragged lines, the babies spend more time looking at the bull's-eye than the zigzags. They like novelty, too, especially if the newcomer comes wrapped in orange or electric blue.

By seven months, as her vision sharpens, Josie will spend as much as 50 percent of her waking-and-exploring time studying the panorama of fixed objects around her. Each object is visually examined and fitted into her pictured world. She notices when a new object is introduced and when one is moved or changed. People are still a favorite, but their familiarity loses out to other attractions. They now get about 30 percent of Josie's attention. Animals like the family spaniel and the robins outside her window get another 20 percent.

DO YOU SEE WHAT I SEE?

Infants are not only fascinated by looking into your eyes, but by what your eyes are looking at. As early as three months, they can follow your eyes as your gaze shifts right or left— even if only the eyes move while the head stays still. You'll see their eye focus swing in the same direction as yours, and they'll follow your gaze even though they can't see what you're looking at.

By tracking your gaze, they are saying, "I want to know what you're looking at." They won't like it, however, if you keep your eyes averted. Like adults, babies are put off by someone who won't look them in the eye. Experiments have shown that infants smile significantly less at a face whose eyes are trained left or right compared to a face with a direct gaze. Someone who peeks at them from the corners of the eye, with the head turned, is not well liked either.

Tracking another's gaze is more evidence of intersubjectivity, the "like me" commonality that links baby and adult. That link will strengthen as the months go by.

But when Baby does look you in the eye now, it's often with a purpose. "Look where I'm looking. See what I'm seeing." Josie will turn her eyes toward the music box by the bed, then look toward you to see if you, too, are looking at the box. "Do you see that?" It's your cue to catch the direction of her gaze, look at the box, and perhaps pick it up and wind it. "That's Josie's music box," you say, being sure to mention her name. "Hear Josie's music box play 'Rockabye Baby'." You might even hum along to the tinkle and rhythm of the box.

Sounds increasingly capture Josie's attention now, too. And not just the loud bangs and slams or passing ambulances that startled her earlier. From birth, she would turn her head in the direction of her mother's voice. She is still tuned to the rhythms and intonations of her mother's voice, but you will now see that she is also taken by the hum of the vacuum cleaner or the lilt of radio music. She tries to fit those sounds together with the rest of her world, and likes to initiate sounds herself. She begins to associate what she sees with the sound it makes (and often how it tastes). The squeak of her doll or the lapping of her rubber bath toy produces squeals of delight. The researcher Philippe Rochat calls this transformation "the two-month revolution." Josie's actions until now have been primarily concerned with what might be called the survival instinct. Her world has been one of feeding, sleeping, bathing, and diaper changing. Now she is moving beyond those basics. As long as early needs are met, she will be focused less on primitive needs and wants and more on exploring and figuring out the complex world she's been born into—as well as the people and objects that populate it.

BEHIND THE SIGNS

Trading Spaces

Once upon a time expectant parents, with great anticipation, papered and painted their nurseries in traditional pinks, pale yellows, and baby blues. Soft shapes, lacy details, and pastel tones were favored in nursery décor for decades. Today, well-informed parents understand that junior enjoys a more colorful palette and that strong shapes with bold definition are much more interesting to his developing eyes. Consider orange, red, and electric blue. Consider black-bordered graphic shapes such as bull's-eyes. Remember, beauty is in the eye of the beholder, and Baby's eyes will eat this up!

FOR CRYING OUT LOUD

HOW TO INTERPRET YOUR BABY'S CRIES

*T*he wailing sound coming from newborn Brianna's crib immediately gets your attention, even though it's 2am. It starts with a few slurping, restless notes, followed by the first tentative "Waah." Then come more "Waah"s, louder, closer together, and higher in pitch. By now you are probably fully awake and at cribside, knowing it's feeding time. But if you're not that quick afoot, the serenade will continue in both volume and duration until you nervously or frantically—or resignedly—intercede. And even though your nurturing actions get Brianna fed and the cries stopped, you know that there are more to come and that crying will be Brianna's signature means of communication for the next year. Or more.

Why Don't Guatemalan Babies Cry?

Babies in the rural and mountainous areas of Central and South America ride in a sling on their mothers' backs. The result is that Mom can feel every twitch and wriggle of the baby's body. When he's hungry, his movements and fussiness tell her so. He doesn't have to cry to remind her. When she sleeps, he sleeps with her, and of course, she quickly knows when he needs a change. Babies in the developed world are more often isolated in nurseries, or in cribs or playpens. They have to tune up their vocal cords to announce their needs and wants.

"Babies cry," one prominent researcher has written. "That's their job." Indeed, the American Academy of Pediatrics says a normal healthy newborn will cry for one to four hours a day, and that each cry carries a message. The word "infant" is derived from the Latin for "without speech," which is not, one must remember, the same as "silent." Most babies come into the world with a hearty cry, the usefulness of which is twofold: it assures parents and obstetricians that the newcomer is healthy and also fills the tiny lungs with oxygen. In the past, doctors often induced this cry—and with it the first breath—with a vigorous slap on the buttocks to get the baby tuned up and breathing rhythmically. That high-pitched "birth cry" is distinctive, but it will be followed by more crying over the next hours, days, weeks, and months as the baby uses his voice to express all manner of wants, feelings, thoughts, and discomforts, and to convey his reaction to external and internal stimuli. Human babies, incidentally, are not alone in their throaty performance. Infants' cries resemble those of some of our fellow mammals and serve similar purposes. Researchers say human crying occurs on the same wavelength and intervals as the mewing of kittens, and often use kittens in their research to explore human crying. Monkeys are notable criers, too.

THE COLICKY CRY—IS THERE A MESSAGE?

Some babies cry and cry and cry. Often the crying occurs at about the same time every day, usually late afternoon, and can go on for hours. The crying may be accompanied by a drawing up of the legs to the chest, balled-up fists, a beet-red face, and tight-shut eyes. The nonstop screaming can terrify a caregiver because she can't fathom the reason for the crying and nothing she does seems to stop it.

Colic is the name usually given to this situation. About 20 percent of babies are described as colicky, but pediatricians say there is a distinction between colicky babies and those who just cry a lot—a fine line not always visible to frazzled parents. Pediatricians usually diagnose colic by the so-called Rule of Three: A normal, healthy baby is considered colicky when he cries for at least three hours a day, three days a week, for three weeks in a row. Oddly, the baby may just cry normally during the day, when hungry or wet, but then explode with seeming rage later.

There is no agreement on what causes colic or on how to deal with it. The only agreement is that, to the vast relief of harried parents, it seems to be confined to the first three months

of life. Some blame it on intestinal upsets or digestive gas, noting that the baby's abdomen may seem distended and the drawn-up legs might indicate pain. Others say the causes are psychological: a colic outburst may be a reaction to tension and hubbub in the house. The fact that colic disappears with time leads to the popular explanation that it reflects some form of neurological change. And some, like Dr. Barry Lester of the Colic Clinic at Brown University, blame all of the above.

The treatments for colic are similarly elusive. Rocking, cradles, swings, and any kind of rhythmic motion have been championed as cures since antiquity. The steady hum of a vacuum cleaner works sometimes. So does strapping the child into the infant chair and placing the chair atop an operating clothes dryer. If that fails, some parents bundle the squalling infant into the car and go for a drive.

One other point of agreement: Colic is not a form of communication. No matter how much mothers or caregivers blame themselves for neglecting the child or mistreating him, colic is not a message of protest. The colicky baby isn't trying to tell you anything.

First-time parents may think that a cry is a cry is a cry. In a sense, that's true. Crying is ordinary, normal, and healthy. A leather-lunged infant is a robust infant. But there are different types of cries, differing in pitch, rhythm, and acoustical properties. They carry different messages and differ from baby to baby. Indeed, your own newborn has her own unique cry, quite recognizable from others.

Researchers in Sweden and Finland have cooperated in a thirty-year study of infant crying. They have observed thousands of babies, tracking and recording their cries and correlating them with various stimuli, such as the temporary pain that might occur by harmlessly snapping a rubber band at the baby's foot. In the first few months, Baby cries largely for physiological reasons—because she is hungry or in pain, or perhaps because she's too hot or too cold, or because she has a wet diaper. The message is "Ouch!" or "I feel yucky," or "Come feed me." But gradually crying occurs for more sophisticated reasons. A seven-month-old's message can be "That scares me!" (fear); "I can't reach that toy!" (frustration); "Come play with me." (need for attention); "I'm tired." (sleepiness); or "Stop! That's enough!" (overstimulation).

At first, babies' cries are purely reflexive. Baby doesn't think, "Gee, look at that clock! It's time for my feeding. I'd better yell and get Mom over here." Rather an internal signal responsive to her needs sets off an instinctive crying mechanism, which forces air up through the windpipe, across the vocal cords and "Waaah!" results. Using sophisticated and computerized technology, researchers in Europe and the United States have recorded and measured the acoustical properties of crying. Their tonal frequency normally registers between 350 and 500 hertz. The average frequency computes to 440 hertz. A Hungarian researcher, gifted with perfect pitch, translated the cries as the note B-natural on the musical scale. That's close to the A orchestras use for tuning up.

Cries are a product of the respiratory system. Each cry is an upward blast of air from the lungs across the vocal cords, after which the crier has to pause and replenish the air supply. Hence the fluctuating "wah-wah-wah," each "wah" consuming eight to ten seconds, with a break for intake. And although it may seem like more when heard in the wee small hours, the volume of a baby's cries is usually about 85 decibels, putting it in the class of an unmuffled truck. (However, some cries have been recorded as high as 117 decibels.) Cries seldom go on for hours on end, as parents sometimes feel they do. It's rare that crying in a normal, healthy baby continues uninterrupted beyond five minutes, and it almost never lasts as long as ten.

BEHIND THE SIGNS

Researchers recording every whimper have found that Baby arrives with only two types of cries. There is a pained cry—a high-pitched, quavering outburst immediately alarming to parents—and a basic cry, used for all other purposes, from hunger to wet diapers. By two months, though, as vocal cords develop, Baby begins to realize that she can produce cries at whim and can use vocalization to get results. Over the next few months, she frequently lets go simply to notify the world that she's angry, frustrated, sleepy, or just lonely.

Crying Guru

Dr. Barry Lester has devoted more than thirty years to understanding crying and colicky infants on an international scale, and has become perhaps the leading expert in this field. He traveled to the Guatemalan highlands in the 1970s for a research project, and heard pitiful malnourished babies whose piercing cries indicated brain damage from lack of protein. Back home, he plunged into the field of neonatology, the care of the newborn. He has specialized in research and diagnosis of brain-damaged infants whose mothers used cocaine and other hard drugs, and, most recently, methamphetamines.

Baby Fact

A breast-feeding mother can recognize her baby's cries, and so can her body. The infant's cries, unique to him, trigger his mother's milk letdown reflex and prepare her for nursing.

At first, parents have a difficult time distinguishing one cry from another. Which wail constitutes an emergency? Which cry can wait for attention? With time, experience, and good listening skills, you can learn to interpret the cry's message. Sometimes, of course, the reason is obvious. When Baby shrieks at the pediatrician's first immunization shots, you recognize that the outcry means, "Ouch! That hurts!" At 2am, when you hear slurping noises from the crib, followed by a tentative whine, and then a short, explosive cry that increases in volume, you have only to look at the clock to get the message that it is feeding time. Definitely an "I'm hungry" cry.

Here is a helpful guide to a baby's cry repertoire and how to interpret what you hear.

Tummy Troubles

When a baby cries a half hour or so after feeding, chili con carne may be to blame. That's because spices ingested in a breast-feeding mother may show up in the breast milk, causing gas or other mild intestinal upset. Pediatricians usually advise mothers to minimize their intake of spicy foods when breast-feeding.

Baby Fact

Although it may seem longer to parents, non-colicky babies rarely cry longer than ten minutes at a stretch.

1. THE HOWL

WHAT YOU HEAR:
A loud, long, shrill cry coming suddenly and unexpectedly. A pause for breath, and then another explosive cry, louder and more insistent, lacking in melody or rhythm. Looking into the crib, you may see a wide-open mouth, a tense body, feet drawn up ,and arms pinned to the sides.

WHAT IT MEANS
"Something really hurts!"

WHAT TO DO
Get there fast. Look for quick explanations. Has something harmful fallen into the crib? Is she rubbing her ear, which could indicate an earache? Check for a fever. Call the pediatrician.

2. THE RHYTHMIC CRY

WHAT YOU HEAR:
Fussiness, some twitching from the crib, a glottal or guttural sound in the throat, a first cry or whine, then rhythmic, wavering crying.

WHAT IT MEANS
"I'm hungry!"

WHAT TO DO
Offer the breast or bottle. If it's not Baby's regular feeding hour, the explanation may be intestinal gas: pick him up, hold him to your shoulder, and burp him.

3. THE WHINE

WHAT YOU HEAR:
Fussiness, followed by rather thin crying, then an arrhythmic cry that fluctuates in pitch and volume. You may hear the sound of fingers being sucked. At the cribside, you may see her rub her eyes or bat her ears.

WHAT IT MEANS
"I'm sleepy!"

WHAT TO DO
If it's nap time and she is in her crib, wait and see if the crying subsides. If it does, check on her and make sure she's warm or cool enough. If she's playing actively with you or a sibling, this type of crying may mean overstimulation—she has had enough! Pick her up, hold her, and soothe her until the crying ends and she calms down.

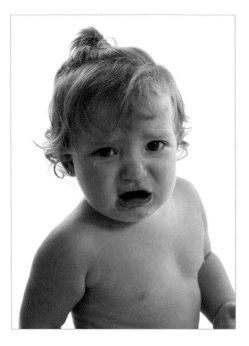

4. THE WHIMPER

WHAT YOU HEAR:
A nasal, weak cry, similar to the pain cry in pitch and suddenness, but with less volume and sometimes of a lower pitch. Pauses for a breath, then the cry resumes, sometimes more feebly. You may see that her face is flushed.

WHAT IT MEANS
"I feel sick!"

WHAT TO DO
Check for immediate signs of illness, such as fever or flushed face, drawn-up legs indicating abdominal pain, rubbing of the ears (ear infection), or diarrhea. Hold and soothe the baby. Call the pediatrician.

5. THE SHRIEK

WHAT YOU HEAR:
A sudden, loud, piercing cry, a sharp intake of breath, then another cry, increasingly piercing.

WHAT IT MEANS
"Something frightened me!"

WHAT TO DO
Go quickly to Baby, pick him up, and soothe him. Look for the cause and correct it. (He may simply have been startled by a loud noise.) In a ten- to twelve-month-old, a continuous fear cry may be caused by separation anxiety: "Mom has gone away. Is she coming back?"

6. THE WAIL

WHAT YOU HEAR:
A loud wail, similar to the pain cry, beginning more gradually but continuing. Often accompanied by wriggling and movement, as though trying to get comfortable.

WHAT IT MEANS
"Change me!"

WHAT TO DO
Check Baby's bottom. In these days of absorbent diapers, wetness alone is seldom a cause for discomfort. Examine for redness, soreness, or diaper rash, and treat accordingly. You may want to leave off diapers until the soreness heals.

7. THE EXHAUSTED SOB

WHAT YOU HEAR:
A long, hard cry, usually at bedtime, that seems
to resist calming.

WHAT IT MEANS
"I've had enough for one day!"

WHAT TO DO
Beforehand, watch for indications of
overstimulation—turning away or nervous
twitching—especially when Baby has been playing
with siblings. Pick up Baby, hold and soothe him,
which may require ten minutes or more.

8. THE DISCOMFORT CRY

WHAT YOU HEAR:
A loud, clear, continuing cry, rising and falling,
but with a definite rhythm.

WHAT IT MEANS
"I'm cold!" or "I'm hot!"

WHAT TO DO
Babies are sensitive to heat or cold. Strangely
enough, the "I'm cold!" cry can be self-correcting.
Crying generates heat, which raises the
temperature. If the baby seems overheated,
remove blankets or some clothing.

9. THE OUTBURST

WHAT YOU HEAR:
An angry, sudden outburst, a pause for breath, and a second outburst. Similar in tone and rhythm to the overstimulation cry.

WHAT IT MEANS
"I'm really mad!" or "I'm really frustrated!"

WHAT TO DO
This is not an emergency. Survey the scene. In babies who can sit or crawl, this cry may indicate frustration because he can't reach or grasp a desired object. In a baby just beginning to stand, the crying may mean, "I've figured out how to stand, now how do I get down?" If he's frustrated, offer him the desired object or help him complete the challenging task, whatever it may be.

10. THE RHYTHMIC SOB

WHAT YOU HEAR:
A low-level, imploring cry, rhythmic and insistent.

WHAT IT MEANS
"I'm lonely and feel neglected. Come and get me!"

WHAT TO DO
A knowledgeable parent will say, "Oh, that's her attention-getting cry!" knowing that Baby, confined to her crib, is envious of the good times she's sure are happening in the living room. She wants to be picked up and join the fun. The next step is up to you.

ABOUT FACE

A GUIDE TO UNDERSTANDING BABY'S FACIAL EXPRESSIONS

*Y*ou've taken away three-month-old Isaiah's teddy bear, you meanie, and he doesn't like it one bit. His face shows it. He draws down his eyebrows, his lips are pressed together into a straight line, and his cheeks are rapidly turning crimson, beet red. He's frustrated. He's plain mad.

Long before Isaiah can send more sophisticated messages using arms or hands, his face expresses basic, simple communication. The contours of the chin, the set of the eyes, the movements of the brows declare his thoughts and feelings almost as well as words ever could. When he's surprised or scared, for instance, his gaping mouth forms a capital letter 'O'. As in the famous Edvard Munch painting *The Scream*, wide-open, startled eyes emphasize his abrupt astonishment. When he's upset or distressed by something like a wet and uncomfortable diaper, the mouth turns down, the eyebrows go up, the eyes fill and pour out tears, as rhythmic sobs rack his little body. When you clown for him and he enjoys your funny faces, he breaks into a wide grin of pleasure.

The baby's face contains twenty-five different sets of muscles, spliced together and orchestrated by the brain's motor cortex. Starting in the early days

BEHIND THE SIGNS

Baby's Facial Timetable

Here's when you can expect your baby to show different facial expressions:

BIRTH: Interest, Distress, Startlement

SIX WEEKS: Happiness

THREE TO FOUR MONTHS: Surprise, Pleasure

FIVE TO NINE MONTHS: Anger, Fear, Disgust, "Dis-smell", Enjoyment, Shame

NINE TO TWELVE MONTHS: Boredom, Anxiety, Anticipation

of life, these muscles work together to express all kinds of feelings and emotions, as researchers have demonstrated by videotaping with high-speed film. Muscle action is triggered when stimuli are picked up by the senses and are processed across the brain, setting off a neural response that tells the eyebrows to pull down in a frown of annoyance or the corners of the mouth to turn up when you say, "Hello, Babeee!" The facial-expression network is clearly present from birth and is part of the baby's survival defense. The alarmed look that follows a sudden loud noise is designed to tell the baby's protector that he feels threatened.

Baby Fact:

All babies love mirrors. Put your little one in front of his reflection and watch him practice his repertoire of facial gestures.

MIRROR IMAGE

Come face to face with your newborn. Stick out your tongue at him. You'll find that he will stick out his tongue, too! The natural mimic will copy you even though he has never seen his tongue and doesn't even know he has one. Andrew Meltzoff of the University of Washington made this astonishing discovery in 1977, and although most scientists couldn't believe it at the time, it has since been reproduced by other researchers many times. If you look into Baby's eyes and blink at him, he'll blink back, too. And if you open your mouth wide into an O shape, you'll find yourself looking right down your baby's throat, just like he's looking down yours.

BEHIND THE SIGNS

Feel My Pain?

You can tell when your four-month-old is happy, sad, or distressed just by looking at her face. But when Baby looks in your face, can she tell what you're feeling? Many researchers think she can. A four-month-old can readily distinguish between a happy face and a sad face, and she can reproduce whichever expression she sees before her. But does looking sad make her feel sad? Does imitating a happy face make her feel happy? No one has yet devised an experiment that would successfully answer these questions, but many scientists are trying.

Babies, like adults, have an impressive array of facial expressions, any of which can be switched on at a moment's notice. A lively debate among researchers concerns the precise number; for example, some feel that the expression sometimes classified as "alarm" is actually just a more extreme expression of the basic category "surprise," which exists from birth. Remember, too, that all babies' faces are different and thus their expressions seem different. Moreover, the range of expressions increases over time as the baby develops and gains new experiences. Take, for instance, six-month-old Carlos, who can sit upright in his high chair and look around, and eleven-month-old Lucy, who is taking her first steps on wobbly legs. They see a completely different world, and have different reactions and facial expressions than newborn Nick, still lying in his crib and only sleeping, eating, and filling up diapers. The expressions—and the reactions they indicate—also operate on a kind of continuum: interest leads to excitement, for instance, and anger to uncontrollable rage.

Child psychiatrist Paul Holiger of Chicago has classified nine telltale infant facial expressions common to almost all babies in the first year of life. He terms them interest, enjoyment, surprise, distress, anger, fear, shame, disgust, and dis-smell. (Others would add boredom, sadness, and overstimulation.) The first three, he notes, signify "Fun" and the other six are calls for help. There are more negative than positive expressions because it is more important for the helpless human infant to signal when he is threatened than when he is secure.

Here's how to recognize each common facial expression and its corresponding message.

1. INTERESTED FACE

WHAT YOU SEE
Baby is looking intently at an object just beyond his reach, maybe a cup on a nearby table. His mouth is slightly opened. His eyebrows are raised, and his head is cocked as if listening, too. He maintains his eye focus for several minutes, as if studying the object.

WHAT IT MEANS
"That little cup is really fascinating!"

WHAT TO DO
Encourage his interest by naming the object: "Oh, that's a cup, John. Isn't it pretty?" If the cup is breakable, pick it up, show it to him, and then move it to a safer place.

2. JOYFUL FACE

WHAT YOU SEE
You've just made some funny faces for Baby, and he's broken into a wide and engaging smile. His eyes are bright, his eyebrows and whole face relaxed. He has cute baby dimples in his chubby cheeks.

WHAT IT MEANS
"Oh, that was fun! Do it again!"

WHAT TO DO
Smile in return and enjoy the moment right along with him.

3. SURPRISED FACE

WHAT YOU SEE
O! A sudden noise startled Baby and her mouth forms a big, round oval. Up go her eyebrows, wrinkling her forehead. Her eyes are opened wide and blinking. She may look a little apprehensive, even fearful.

WHAT IT MEANS
"Oh! That startled me. I wasn't expecting that!"

WHAT TO DO
Reassure her verbally ("That was loud, wasn't it? It startled me, too. But now it's over and everything's all right.") and with a hug if needed.

4. DISTRESSED FACE

WHAT YOU SEE
Baby's stuffed tiger is missing. As you fruitlessly hunt for it, he becomes more and more upset, shown by arched eyebrows, and his mouth turned down at the corners. Tears seep from the corners of his scrunched-up, almost closed eyes. The little body racks with sobs.

WHAT IT MEANS
"This is terrible for me! I am so upset!"

WHAT TO DO
Hold him, console him, and wipe away the tears. Try to distract him with another toy. Assure him that Tiger will be found or replaced.

5. ANGRY FACE

WHAT YOU SEE
Something has set your six-month-old off. She's frowning, making her eyes narrow. She clenches her jaw and presses her lips together. Her face is beet red.

WHAT IT MEANS
"Boy, am I mad!"

WHAT TO DO
You'll probably have to tough it out and just wait for the storm clouds to dissipate. You want her to know that it's okay to be angry sometimes. Often, the emotion is directed more at herself than others: she may be showing frustration because she couldn't reach a toy or play a game. If you can identify the cause of her frustration and correct it, do so.

6. FEARFUL FACE

WHAT YOU SEE
A child with his eyes wide open and staring, under knitted brows. His skin looks pale and cold. He's trembling, and his hair is standing up.

WHAT IT MEANS
"I'm really afraid!"

WHAT TO DO
Rather than deny the fear ("Oh, don't be a baby. That wasn't something to be afraid of.") try to see it from the child's point of view. ("That clown was kind of scary, wasn't it?") Remember that events that frighten one young child might be dismissed as routine by another. Fear is a powerful emotion, setting off the self-protective fight-or-flight reaction.

7. ASHAMED FACE

WHAT YOU SEE
Contrition. The child's eyes are downcast, the eyelids lowered. The face droops, and the head hangs down in the "I plead guilty" posture.

WHAT IT MEANS
"Please don't be mad at me."

WHAT TO DO
Be forgiving and consoling, but try to convey to your child that certain behaviors are not acceptable.

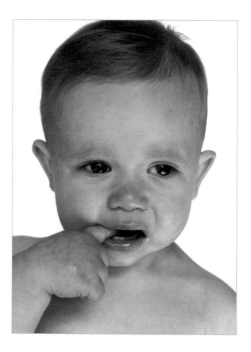

8. DISGUSTED FACE

WHAT YOU SEE
A stuck-out tongue and a protruding upper lip. Narrowed eyes under pulled-down eyelids. And the giveaway: a wrinkled, upturned nose.

WHAT IT MEANS
"Yuck! That is revolting!"

WHAT TO DO
Disgust is believed to be a biologically primitive and protective emotion, designed to keep the body from ingesting harmful substances. But it may just be your baby's particular reaction to a spoonful of strained spinach. Try offering the spinach again at another meal, or substitute another nourishing vegetable.

9. SMELLY FACE

WHAT YOU SEE
An upwardly crinkling nose and a curled upper lip. The baby turns her head away from the unpleasantness.

WHAT IT MEANS
"Ugh! Something stinks!"

WHAT TO DO
Like disgust, "dis-smell" is thought of as a basic defense mechanism, protecting the child from inhaling noxious or harmful substances. Correct the problem if you can. But if the smell comes from a substance like a needed medicine or a necessary food, you may have to forge ahead.

HANDY DANDY

BABY'S HAND GESTURES AND MOVEMENTS BEGIN TO HAVE MEANING

WHAT BABY DOES
Wiggles the fingers and curls the palms.

WHAT BABY MEANS
"Look at my hands. I am trying to tell you something."

WHAT YOU SHOULD NOTICE
Hand movements are starting to matter.

Week-old Sam has some brand-new toys. They're called his hands. He's discovered them accidentally but now he's entranced. Those fascinating little palms, with the five tiny attachments that bend and fold and curl, absolutely intrigue Sam. He moves them up to his face and sometimes, when he gets lucky with his aim, in front of his eyes. There he can study them, turning them this way and that, for a thorough inspection. He can taste them too. They find their way into his mouth, sometimes after several attempts. They will return there quite often. And they will be an endless source of entertainment.*

To Sam, these moist, soft, amusing things are something of a miracle. They just pop up in front of his face or turn up between his gums of their own aimless volition. Or so developmental psychologists once believed. How would someone little more than hours old, with a brain still developing, know anything about hands? Or be able to recognize these fascinating things as his own, as part of Sam? How would a newborn be able to coordinate hand and arm movement to bring them within scanning and chewing range?

The answer is proprioception, and it comes with the newborn package. Proprioception is a mysterious, inborn quality in all of us, as well as in many of our fellow animals. Proprioception allows us to locate our body parts, where they are situated at a given movement, what they are doing and where they are moving, and how they are bending and flexing and connecting to each other. We don't have to look or feel for them to get that information. You don't have to check out every arm, finger, or shoulder blade. As you read this, your arms and hands are probably propping the book at correct visual range, your hindquarters are plopped into a chair, and your head is upright with eyes pointed toward the printed page. Without looking or thinking about it, you know the positioning of every limb and joint. In fact, proprioception is so inborn and unconscious that fitness trainers have to urge their clients to make a deliberate effort to "feel" the configuration of their bodies.

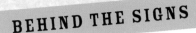

Living Hand to Mouth

At twenty minutes old, a baby has been photographed with a hand in his mouth. But actually, hand and mouth may have been together before that; fetuses have been shown sucking thumbs or hands while still in the womb and some have been born with bruises or sore spots on thumbs or wrists. The hand–mouth affinity is apparently programmed from the start, an example of complex coordination. The baby moves his hand upward, and instinctively opens his mouth in anticipation. As the hand nears its goal, the mouth opens wider, ready to receive it, then closes around it with an air of Mission Accomplished.

YOUR LITTLE EXPLORER

Hands are to baby Sam what sailing vessels were to Vasco da Gama and Christopher Columbus: a means to exploring the outer boundaries of their known world. By three months, he can grasp objects handed to him, and at five months he can reach toward them. At first, he will start out by swiping at or raking in the desired objects, but he will soon be able to hold them with palm and thumb. By seven or eight months he will begin to use thumb and forefinger together in a pincers grip. By twelve months he will have mastered the grip sufficiently to pick up tiny objects. So begins self-feeding. Now Sam can pick up bits of food and guide them to his mouth. (Or toss them away in distaste, to your dismay!) With his coordinated reach and grasp, he can take hold of intriguing objects and scoop them up for closer examination. He gives each one the three-pronged test of touch, sight, and taste. You'll see him hold the object, pass it from hand to hand as though testing it for weight, bring it up to his face for closer scrutiny, then give it the ultimate test by chewing on it. A baby's mouth, one researcher has said in scientific language, "is the primary locus of object exploration." Translation: the mouth is the first place Baby puts things to figure out what they are. Even inedible objects get the taste test. Taste, touch, and sight are an infant's coordinated tools of exploration and information gathering.

The Age of Discovery also introduces a new stage of communication, of secret language. Finding new things to explore, the baby begins to hold them up for adults to admire, identify, and explain.

The same thing goes for Sam. Sam doesn't know what those funny things called hands are, and he's much too young to understand the word. But when the hands move in front of his face, he can detect that they are part of him and where they are, right now. He knows at some basic level that they belong to him. Initially, their positioning seems almost random, just an accident of his wildly flailing around. But soon he gains some control over the pesky things. He learns to clasp them together, move them where he can examine them more minutely, chew on them, or taste them. When Sam is given a rattle to hold or a bottle with its nourishment, he can use his hands to grasp the rattle or cling to the bottle. And ultimately he learns to use hands and fingers to reach out to and communicate with the world.

Baby Fact:

Hand-eye coordination, even in its simplest form, is a learned skill for Baby. It is not until she approaches six months old that she can consistently focus on an object and grasp it with her hand—although she has been practicing this feat from about two months old.

The First Taste of Exploration

A newborn quickly begins to raise his hand to his mouth. But when does he realize that he can use his mouth to get a better understanding of that object in his hand? Philippe Rochat of Emory University in Atlanta attempted to find out. He placed a rubber teether in the hand of a newborn. The baby regularly put the empty hand in his mouth and curiously gripped the teether with the other hand while exploring it with his fingers—but he made no effort to carry it to his mouth. Rochat kept trying, but not until the baby was two months old did he begin bringing the teether in front of his eyes or subject the teether to the taste test.

THE SECRET LANGUAGE OF BABIES

Hands and fingers, along with facial expressions and crying, will be Sam's first line of communication until he begins to master the quirkiness of language. Even then, he will use fingers and hands to emphasize speech or send messages for the rest of his life. Watch a hungry diner summon a waiter or two friends greet with a handshake. Yet long before these sophisticated hand gestures become routine, at the earliest outset of life, the hands are already used to connect with others. Offer a finger to a newborn and he will quickly curl tiny fingers around it in return. Imaging devices that can look into the womb show us fetuses moving individual fingers and curling hands. Researchers have even detected the fetus extending the index finger as if pointing to some interesting occurrence or reaching out toward something. Whether this movement can be construed as a genuine effort to point is, to say

the very least, uncertain; if so, it might indicate that pointing at an interesting thing is an inborn action, not learned or acquired.

Baby Fact:

Research has shown that the more an infant is exposed to interesting objects, the quicker her hand-eye coordination will develop.

BODY LANGUAGE 101

COMMUNICATION THROUGH WINDMILLING AND OTHER MOVEMENTS

WHAT BABY DOES
Revolves the arms in a windmill motion.

WHAT BABY MEANS
"I'm really excited about this!"

WHAT YOU SHOULD NOTICE
*Baby can now anticipate when a good thing
(or an unpleasant thing) is about to happen.*

It's a bright sunny day and as you walk across the nursery to fetch Alisha for her feeding, the sunshine throws your shadow across her crib. Instantly, you're aware of a flurry of activity behind the crib bars. Your two month-old is wagging her arms, flapping them in the air, not exactly waving to you but kind of revolving them like the vanes of a windmill. Obviously Alisha is glad to see you. Or at least she recognizes feeding time.

Baby Fact:

Responding to Baby's gestures helps to minimize his frustration and tension. Babies are happiest when they feel they are communicating, when their gestures get some reaction.

Those churning, windmilling arms will be Alisha's all-purpose form of communication while she's on her back, in a supine position, in the crib, and even afterward, when she can sit erect and conduct a point-by-point survey of her neighborhood. They will indeed inform you that Alisha is excited, happy to see you, welcoming your presence, and perhaps anticipating the nourishment that your presence signifies. But other times the rotating windmill may convey a different message entirely. Particularly when accompanied by a crimson, scrunched-up face, the full windmill mode may indicate frustration, fear, or surprise. A sudden loud noise may start the arms whipping around, and when she's really upset the legs will join in. With all four limbs in action, Alisha can drum up a perfect storm of protest.

Baby Fact:

A baby's body develops from the top down, from head to toes, and from the torso outward. Notice that Baby will learn to use her arms before her hands, and her hands before her fingers.

In terms of growing command over musculature, a baby develops from top to bottom. First head and neck muscles strengthen, and Alisha can lift her head off the mattress to look around. Next come shoulders and arms, then the trunk and legs. Full control and use of the arms and hands won't come until she is seven months old and able to sit upright, fully extend the arms, and flex the fingers. That will sprout a repertoire of gestures and movements and a whole new and improved vocabulary of secret language.

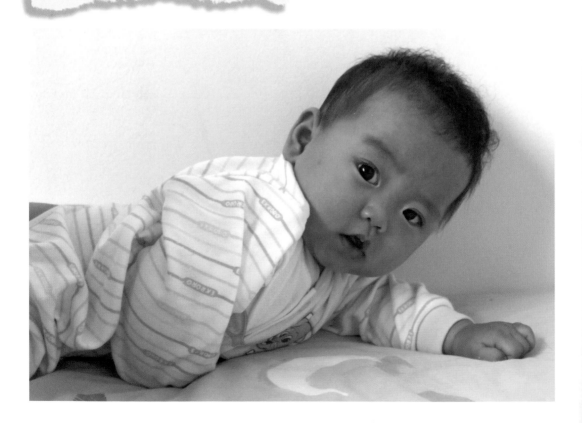

Meanwhile, the little communicator will use her arms in expressive ways other than just windmilling. Strike a resounding pan near the crib and—along with an outraged cry of surprise—a startled Alisha is likely to draw her arms tightly against her body and ball up her fists, trembling with fright. At the first sight of a new, brightly colored toy, the arms will wave in an expression of pure delight. If she drops the toy somewhere out of reach, she may hammer on the mattress in protest, wailing all the while. When she is impatient for lunch, an older Alisha may pound—and pound and pound—on her high chair tray.

Alisha's full-body performance points to another stage in her emotional growth. Her developing memory opens up her mastery of anticipation and association. Each new experience triggers recollections of similar past experiences, and leads her to anticipate what will come next. She knows that certain events predict future events. She hears the crunch of gravel in the driveway and the sound of the car engine shutting down, and knows that those noises mean that Daddy or Mommy has come home. Instantly, the chubby arms go into their windmill mode. Some other examples of anticipation and greeting may be less popular. When she sees the feeding spoon approaching with a mouthful of disliked food, she can anticipate the taste from remembered experience, and move the arms in front of her in a clear blocking message of, "No way! None of that for me."

Bye Bye Baby

The first words Baby understands may be related to, and accompanied by, hand movements. "Bye bye," with its wagging fingers and a broad smile, is an early addition to the understood vocabulary. "Say 'bye bye' to Grandma" cues the little grandchild to wave and smile. "Peekaboo," the fun now-you-see-me-now-you-don't game, is another early understood set of words. With time and repetition, a baby understands that spoken words can have multiple meanings. "Bye bye" isn't just a farewell wave, but also refers to going places: "Now it's time to go bye bye."

GOTTA DANCE

HOW LEGS AND FEET PLAY A ROLE IN BABY'S SECRET LANGUAGE

WHAT BABY DOES

Thumps and kicks his legs and feet.

WHAT BABY MEANS

"I have a message for you."

WHAT YOU SHOULD NOTICE

*The whole body, including the lower half,
is important in Baby's secret language.*

You're approaching two-month-old Amar's crib. He's now at the stage where he's awake more and sleeping less. It's the "quiet alert" state, but the sounds from the crib are anything but quiet. He's not just smiling at you, but also greeting you with upstretched waggling arms, and, yes, down below his legs are engaged in their own flurry of welcoming activity, thrashing and kicking. He's glad to see you from top to bottom and his body language says so.

TINY DANCER

If you hold a newborn upright on his feet, he will reflexively lift his leg as if walking. This step reflex is also called "the dancing reflex." At birth, the baby is tested for this ability, to evaluate not only his reflexes but also his leg strength. If a baby's foot were pricked, his other foot would swing over and try to kick the offending object away. The "dancing reflex" test is also a way to obtain a baby's footprint, a permanent and individual form of identification.

We don't think of legs and feet as being involved in communication, but in Amar's wordless world they play a prominent communicative role. He uses them to convey all kinds of messages, from pleasure to protest. Even as a newborn, he kicked as part of his "I'm hungry" outcry, feet thumping on the crib mattress. Later, an eight-month-old Amar, impatient in his high chair, will recognize that one way to call for his release is to use his feet to beat a loud attention-getting tattoo on the chair legs. An older Amar, performing his first temper tantrum, will use his thrashing legs and vigorous kicks to inform the world that he has been hard done by and is most unhappy about it.

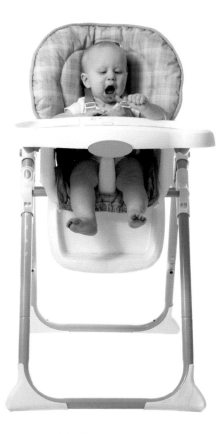

BEHIND THE SIGNS

Testing, Testing, 1 -2 -3

One minute after birth and again at five minutes, a baby's Apgar Score is assessed. The score is simply a quick gauge of the baby's condition at birth. The baby is rated on a scale of zero to two in five categories: heart rate, respiratory effort, muscle tone, color, and response to stimuli. The maximum score for a normal baby is ten.

A very low score, particularly if repeated in the second assessment, calls for immediate medical attention. A score of four to seven at five minutes isn't a cause for action, but is a warning to doctors and parents to watch the baby over the next few days and weeks. Few babies achieve a ten; one doctor jokes that he only gives a ten to children of colleagues as a professional courtesy. Most normal babies score an eight or nine.

🚼 Baby Fact:

About 10 percent of babies take their first step by eleven months; another 10 percent, not until fifteen months. Such a range is normal.

Top Heavy!

Although the secret language of babies does encompass movements of the body, we have seen that facial expressions account for a major portion of messages sent by your little one. One reason for this may be Baby's proportions. Consider this: The average male newborn weighs 7.5 pounds (340 grams) and measures 20 inches (50 cm) long, with females slightly smaller in both categories. However, the baby's head accounts for a quarter of his total length and a third of his weight! These proportions steadily change through infancy and childhood. By adulthood the head comprises less than 10 percent of the body's length, and the legs make up nearly half.

The legs are important to communication in another way. In early infancy, Baby's legs are crooked, bent at the knees, and splayed out sideways rather than directly forward. Try to stand week-old Amar upright and the legs give way. By three to four months his legs are straightening and in an upright position they can bear weight. By nine months he can pull himself to a standing position and even hold that pose for a few seconds. Then comes his first step. Standing and walking, the consequences of increased leg strength, give him a new perspective on the world and lots more to communicate about. He can move himself to objects, reach for them, grasp them, scrutinize them, taste them, and inquire about them. Amar becomes a mobile information-gathering machine. An upright Amar adds whole pages to his secret-language vocabulary.

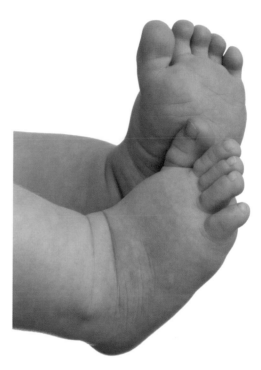

Baby Fact:

If a baby's big toe is extended, chances are good that she is in pain. If the whole foot is stiff and pointing toward the floor, it could indicate acute pain. Discomfort is often expressed by slightly curled toes.

Arms, legs, and body work in synchrony in the secret language of babies. For example, the waggling of angry arms and thumping of protesting legs, plus shakes of the head, may come together to communicate: "I'm mad as hell and I'm not going to take it anymore!" Of course similar movements may also converge to express the exact opposite: enjoyment, delight, and, "I am having so much fun!" In short, vigorous body language generally communicates a passionate message, which could be either positive or negative. As caregiver, you will be aware of context, and therefore also the emotion being expressed, whether over-the-top joy or seething anger!

JUST SAY NO

BABY LEARNS TO EXPRESS DISLIKES

WHAT BABY DOES
*Turns her head away abruptly, tightens her lips,
and waves her arms.*

WHAT BABY MEANS
"No way! I don't like that! Well, maybe."

WHAT YOU SHOULD NOTICE
*Baby is becoming a true individual with her own
particular likes and dislikes but is willing to negotiate.*

Six-month-old Melissa says "No!" Absolutely "No!" It's not a polite "No, thank you," or "Well, maybe; try coaxing me." It's an emphatic refusal. "Do not give me another spoonful of those wretched strained peas." "Do not pick me up and put me to bed." Melissa's head turns away from the advancing spoon, her arms go up to block its progress. Her lips are tightly closed against it. One of those windmilling arms may knock away the spoon and its nasty, mushy, green contents.

An infant's first unmistakable spoken word—to parents' dismay—is very often "No!" At just six months, Melissa can't manage to form that syllable yet. But "no" is very much in her secret language. Her actions make her meaning absolutely clear. She uses her arms, mouth, eyebrows, and facial expressions to accentuate the negative. No parent needs to send out for an interpreter to understand the message. The meaning is as plain as the determined face.

Melissa's reaction is, in fact, a learned response. Almost from birth, babies express their wants, their likes and dislikes, what pleases them or causes them to scrunch up their faces in distaste. The infant learns early that a vigorous swivel of the head or insistent hammering with the hands conveys a "no" message. Mom or Dad is likely to take away that offending spoonful of peas. If the tactic is successful and the peas vanish, she is likely to try it again—and again. No, no, no!

Melissa also learns "No!" from the adults around her. Listen to yourself as she reaches for a forbidden or dangerous object and you say sharply, "No!" In every language "no" or its equivalent is expressed emphatically, in a quick, brusque tone, usually in a deeper tonal register than your normal voice. It may be accompanied by a firm shake of the head and warning, wagging finger, or perhaps a knitting of the brows and a tightening of the lips. To a child that reaction is both attention-getting and a bit scary, but your meaning comes across. Watch Melissa's refusal now and see your own facial expressions mirrored in hers.

"No!" itself usually enters the child's spoken vocabulary somewhere near the first birthday, but it will still be accompanied and underscored—and preceded—by the expressions and gestures of the child's secret language.

Developmentally, another bit of progress is occurring, although a parent may not see "No!" as progress. The neural connections in the infant brain have advanced so that Melissa sees herself as an independent individual, sensitive to likes and dislikes. She recognizes that she's attached to her caregivers, but also that she's a separate individual with her own opinions. Peas? Memory tells her that that green stuff was distasteful, and she makes her feelings clear.

In some polite Asian cultures, it's said, there are 100 different ways of courteously saying "Yes," yet 99 of these expressions actually mean "No" in a passive-aggressive manner. Similarly, in the secret language

Does He Know His Name?

An experiment by Golinkoff and Hirsh-Pasek set out to discover at what age babies begin to recognise and respond to the sound of their own names being spoken. They started by noting the response of each baby when the child's actual name was used. They then used a different with the same stress pattern. Lastly they called out a different name entirely. At four months, most babies responded to their own names; next to names with the same stress pattern; and finally to names with a different pattern. By seven months, they responded only to their own.

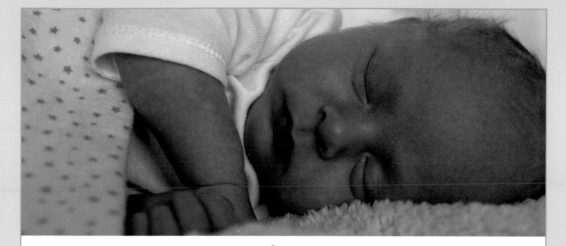

SEEKING THE ANSWERS

Psychologists Roberta Minchnick Golinkoff and Kathy Hirsh-Pasek are longtime collaborators whose pioneering research has led to many insights into how babies develop a secret language and how that leads to the spoken word. Golinkoff, Professor at the University of Delaware, has been focusing on children's language development for more than thirty years. Hirsh-Pasek, Professor and Director of the Infant Language Laboratory at Temple University, is also coprincipal investigator in the U.S. government's Study of Early Child Care, a longitudinal study of how different forms of child care affect children's social, emotional, and intellectual growth.

A particular interest for both of these experts has been how children understand adult speech before they themselves can talk. When they do begin to speak, at best, a single word at a time, can they comprehend and follow strings of words, and, more importantly, the differences among them? Do they know the difference between "Cookie Monster is tickling Big Bird" and "Big Bird is tickling Cookie Monster"? In an ingenious head-turning study using a hidden camera and two video monitors, Golinkoff and Hirsh-Pasek showed that fourteen-month-olds were indeed able to detect the difference by turning in the direction of the correct response. Moreover, they could tell where one sentence ended and another began, and even pick out key words. When Mom holds a long telephone conversation with Cousin Mary and inserts the words, "It's time for Amanda's nap," Amanda knows what's being said. Hirsh-Pasek, a musician herself, has been especially interested in how rhythm and intonation help children understand speech.

Their 2003 book, *Einstein Never Used Flash Cards*, describes how children really learn and decries parents' misguided efforts to build a superbaby with early "learning" methods.

of babies, there are multiple ways of saying "no," but few of them translate to a definitive and emphatic "Never!" If little Melissa could put it into words, "no" might more precisely mean, "Let's discuss this a little," or "Why don't we sit down and negotiate and see if we can come to an agreement we can both live with."

The developmental psychologist Roberta Minchnick Golinkoff of the University of Delaware set out in 1985 to see how often Melissa's seemingly inflexible "no" could be translated as "Let's talk it over." Quite often, she found. Placing Baby in a high chair with Mom beside her, Golinkoff and her assistants concealed themselves (and a video camera) behind a screen and watched while Mom served lunch. Their grainy videotapes of ninety-three lunches record how often the baby's hands, feet, arms, and facial expressions conveyed "No" when Mom offered a spoonful of vegetables, and the eventual outcome of their "dialogue." They counted only those episodes where the baby initiated the "conversation" by pointing, gesturing, or leaning toward the food.

In about half the instances, Baby accepted the food without, or with little, complaint. In the other half, she first refused the spoon. Mom didn't understand the message, chose to misunderstand, or persisted in offering the unwanted food. Baby kept trying, using other techniques, which Golinkoff classified like this:

Repetition (13 percent of episodes): Baby repeated the same signal, usually a little more insistently.

Augmentation (11 percent of episodes): Baby tried additional signals—leaning toward the food, whimpering, and squirming in the chair—to make sure Mom got the point.

Substitution (11 percent of episodes): Instead of the original offering, Baby pointed out a second choice—the bottle or the mashed banana instead of the vegetable.

In 14 percent of episodes Baby flatly rejected all offerings.

Then began the process of negotiation. Both sides kept communicating, hoping to find a common ground, somewhat like political horse trading. Eventually, Baby's signal came through. In 58 percent of cases where he had first refused, he won out, and Mom put down her spoon. In 5 percent of cases the two sides compromised; Baby accepted a little of the dreaded vegetable, and Mom agreed to the cookie. In 7 percent of cases, Mom gave up on the vegetable and substituted a more agreeable offering, like mashed bananas. In 18 percent of cases, it was Baby who chose a substitute, agreeing to the strained peaches instead of the peas. And in the remaining cases, Baby gave in. Both sides recognized, Golinkoff said, that they would negotiate again another day. Discouraged by all this negativity? Don't be. Naturally, babies often say "yes" too, but in a different style. A warm smile usually does it.

LET'S PLAY

OBJECT PERMANENCE LESSONS THROUGH "PEEKABOO" AND "I'M GONNA GET YOU"

WHAT BABY DOES
*Covers her face with a blanket
and then delightedly whisks it off.*

WHAT BABY MEANS
"I see you! This is fun ... let's do it again!"

WHAT YOU SHOULD NOTICE
*Baby now understands that you are there
even when she cannot see you.*

Fun! Janice slyly pulls her "blankie" across her face, hiding her eyes, then whisks it off with a triumphant cry. "Peekaboo! I see you!" you exclaim to more peals of laughter. Then you switch roles. You pull the blanket over your face, hold it there while Janice gurgles in anticipation. "Where's Daddy?" And then you whip it off. "Peekaboo!" More joyous gurgling. Janice, with wide, joyful eyes and upraised brows, brings her hands together in a kind of applause. See, you found me and I found you!

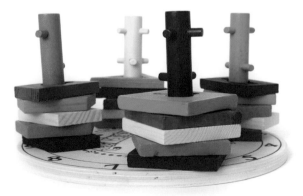

Quite possibly, Adam and Eve played peekaboo with Cain and Abel. Likely the oldest parent-child game around, it's a game that crosses centuries, cultures, nations, and languages. Researchers have documented versions of it among Pacific Islanders, Inuits in the Arctic, Mongolian nomads, and the Chinese.

Peekaboo can be an amusement mainstay as early as four months, but it is more than just an enjoyable game. It also underscores an important lesson in your child's mental development. Before that age, infants are puzzled, sometimes upset, when their teddy bear or favorite caregiver disappears from sight. Teddy and Mommy have completely vanished from baby's radar screen. Where have they gone? Will they ever come back? Do they still exist?

SING-ALONG

Pat-a-cake, pat-a-cake, baker's man. Bake me a cake, as fast as you can! Roll it, and pat it, and mark it with a **B**. And put it in the oven for Baby and me!

Baby Fact:

The earliest traceable publication of the popular nursery rhyme "Pat-a-Cake" is 1698.

Reit-ee, Reit-ee, Kleine Kind

Nursery-rhyme games occur in most every language and culture. Mother Goose's "Ride-a-cock-horse," with a sitting baby bouncing to a nursery jingle on an adult's knee, has its counterpart in European languages. "Reit-ee, reit-ee, kleine kind" ("Ride, ride, little child"), the author's Pennsylvania Dutch grandfather sang to him as a child.

Peekaboo is one way children learn otherwise. When Mom is under the "blankie," she hasn't gone forever. No, indeed, she is very much here, just temporarily hiding under the blanket. Researchers call this discovery the lesson of "object permanence." Just because you can't see the teddy bear anymore, it doesn't mean that it isn't there. And, thankfully, the same goes for Mom!

Another simple and widely played children's game contains a different, but similarly important, lesson. Patty-cake—or pat-a-cake to purists—with its accompanying nursery rhyme, hardly needs explaining. Baby sits on your lap facing you, and you clap your own hands together. Then you reach out and pat baby's upheld palms with your own: your left on Baby's right, Baby's right on your left, and then right to right and left to left, and then another clapping. The lesson here is a fundamental in social conversation: taking turns. As in speech, first it's your turn, then mine. This important lesson will carry over when dialogue begins.

YOU STARTED IT!

Babies start playing games at about four months. You hold a napkin in front of your face, whisk it away, and shout "Peekaboo!" to Baby's squeals of delight. At that stage Baby is just a happy onlooker. You start the game and he joins in. But by eight months he will take the initiative, hiding his own face to get your attention or thrusting his arms up to hear you say, "So big!" In fact, he will start game after game after game—until you're exhausted but he isn't.

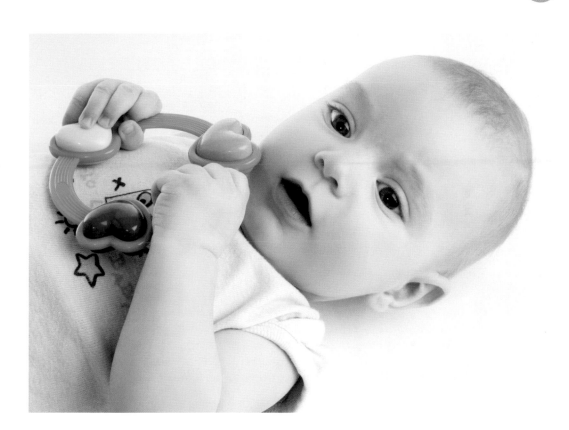

Nursery-rhyme games promote parent-child interaction, too. Baby is ready for them at four months but they go on until she is about to speak her first words. Rhythm and intonation, as taught by "Mother Goose", are important from a developmental point of view, not just in rhyming but also in ordinary, conversational speech. If that's not reason enough to brush up on your "Mother Goose", remember that these games are also, quite simply, a lot of fun—and for both generations!

BABY BUTTERFINGERS

BABY INVENTS A GAME TO KEEP YOUR ATTENTION

WHAT BABY DOES

Drops an object and waits for you to pick it up.

WHAT BABY MEANS

"I'm bored. Let's play!"

WHAT YOU SHOULD NOTICE

Baby is learning to manipulate your behavior.

One morning Charlie knocks his cup off the high chair tray. The seven-month-old wails in the unmistakable cry of infant anguish. An alarmed mom hears the panicky cries, sees the problem, and, with cooing sounds of reassurance, quickly returns the errant object to its aggrieved owner. Before Charlie can really get a grip on the cup, it slips from his grasp and topples to the floor again. More wails. Mom turns back, retrieves the fallen treasure, and hands it back. More cooing and reassurances.

The wails give way to smiles. "Hey, that was fun! Great game! I drop it, she picks it up. I drop it again, she picks it up again." Peals of laughter with each drop-retrieve-drop-retrieve sequence. Each plop of the cup is greeted by a cascade of movements showing what a good time Charlie is having. He gleefully waves his little arms, his kicking legs and feet beat against the chair, and he throws his head back in raucous laughter. What started by accident becomes a bit more deliberate, even sly. Charlie is not only enjoying himself, but he has come up with a way to hold his mom's undivided attention. What more could a seven-month-old ask for? And all this with a simple arm motion: Just extend the arm, open the fingers, and let go. Message delivered. The game goes on and on, down, up, down, up, until Mom's patience wears thin or Charlie gets bored and calls the game off.

🍼 Baby Fact:

Anything tied to baby's neck or wrist presents a strangulation hazard. Although you may feel tempted to try this after retrieving that stray item for the umpteenth time ... don't!

Means To An End

In his scientific *Diary of a Baby*, psychologist Daniel N. Stern describes how the four- to six-month-old recognizes his power to influence events to his liking and then plots ways to bring such events about. The child observes what happens when he performs a certain action, even inadvertently, that brings about a response he favors. So he tries it again, it works, and the stimulus–response pattern—the set of movements—is etched into his brain. Later he will be able to formulate this sequence by using words. But for now, it's a matter of signaling his desires through body language that clearly says, "Hey, Mom, let's have some fun!"

This bit of body language carries an obvious communication: "Hey, Mom, come on over here. Come play with me." It's a message quite familiar—sometimes all too familiar—to almost every parent. But more is going on here than a simple invitation to play games. This small-time sporting event marks an important step in Charlie's development. His body language demonstrates three things about Charlie's growth.

First, his body is saying that Charlie now recognizes that when objects or people vanish from sight, that doesn't mean they're lost forever. Until between four and six months, just the opposite was true. When that precious cup or his mom disappeared, even momentarily, to Charlie's mind, it (or she) was gone for all time. The understanding that things have a presence even when they're absent, an understanding fully formed by seven months, is an important milestone in a baby's growth. Think what it means in your own adult life. You want to count on people or things to be stable even when they're off the radar screen.

BABY HOLD ON

Babies waggle their arms early on, but true coordinated movement doesn't begin until about three months. That's when little Julie can first grip a bottle. By four months she can extend her arm with a fair amount of accuracy to grasp the bottle. A month later she can control arm and finger movements well enough to pick up small objects like the pacifier or bits of food. Dropping them (and throwing them) comes later.

Second, his body movements show that Charlie has developed coordination that he didn't have when he was five months old. It takes advanced cooperation between the central and peripheral nervous systems, the brain and nerves controlling the muscles, plus hand-eye skills to guide that cup from high chair to kitchen floor. Charlie is now coordinated enough to pick up the cup, extend a little arm however awkwardly, calculate the trajectory of the cup's possible descent, open the thumb and fingers in a letting-go motion, track the downward plunge with his eyes, and then punctuate the whole sequence with a come-hither wail or giggle.

Third, Charlie has now learned—maybe, again, to Mom's uplifted eyebrows and furrowed forehead—that he can influence both the people and the things around him. He can make things happen. He can put together a plan involving multiple steps and expect it to work out: "If I do this, Mom will do that, then I'll do this." Step by calculated step. A simple plan by adult standards, but a recognizable plan nonetheless.

Moreover, Charlie has now developed a memory, both short-term and long-term. Conventional wisdom used to purport that babies under a year old couldn't remember what happened a few minutes ago, let alone a few days ago. The dropped cup is gone, gone, lost for all time; Tuesday's game will be forgotten by Wednesday. In this skeptical view, memory doesn't take shape until babies have something to remember. However, the modern, scientific facts show otherwise. In one intriguing experiment, a scientist at the University of Washington showed one-year-old children a fascinating box. The scientist would touch his forehead to the box, and it would light up. But he didn't let the babies touch the box. A week later, he handed the box to the babies, but he didn't do anything with it himself. Guess what happened? The babies immediately touched their foreheads to the box, as if they couldn't wait to see if they could make this strange object glow just as it had the week before.

There's another side to this bit of body language, not always so charming. Babies will often use what they've learned to gain the attention from their caregiver that they crave. Charlie's game is a shining example of this. His message here isn't "Oh, fumble-fingered me. I've lost my cup again. I just can't seem to hold on to it." Rather, it's, "Mom is doing all this other dull stuff and ignoring me. I want her to come here and play. I've been alone long enough." It's all quite cleverly thought out by your budding strategist!

"What's a mother to do?" begs the age-old question. Understandably, you might feel a bit exasperated as the game goes on and on, repeating itself at each high chair seating. Removing the cup altogether isn't an option, because it will only produce more angry wails. But how about removing Baby? Now may be the time to scoop up Charlie for a bath or a sojourn to the backyard, or to distract him with a cracker. Given a seven-month-old's limited attention span—the best estimate is two minutes—the allure of dropping the cup will soon be forgotten, but not for long. Watch that high chair tray tomorrow!

BEYOND GOO-GOO-GA-GA

THE TRUE MEANING OF INTERNATIONAL BABY BABBLE

WHAT BABY DOES

Makes a sound like "dadadada."

WHAT BABY MEANS

"Testing, testing, 1-2-3."

WHAT YOU SHOULD NOTICE

Don't kid yourself—she's not trying to say "Daddy" yet.

ext to Dad sits Sarah in her high chair, addressing the world. She's making long strings of sounds with a vague resemblance to human speech. Not that this is so unusual: She has been cooing, gooing, and gurgling almost since birth. Then a few snorts were thrown in. At about five months she turned to long, penetrating vowel sounds: "eee-eee-eee" and "ooo-oooooo." Recently she has introduced consonants in the mix: "bababa" and "papapa." Tonight she came up with another: "dadada." Elated and excited, the father of the family jumps to his feet. "Did you hear her? She said, 'Dada!' She knows me! Her first word!" And off he runs to call Grandma with the great news.

CROSS-CULTURAL BABBLE

Babies babble in all countries, yet their babbling differs according to the home language. In one test, French experimenters listened to babble of children from English-speaking and French-speaking homes. The experimenters could easily differentiate the French babblers from the English ones by noting the rhythm and intonation of their babble. The voices of French babies, like French adults, rose in inflection at the end of a "speech." English babies' voices tend to soften and drop.

Unfortunately, Dada's glee is probably a bit premature. Beginning between four and five months old, Sarah and her contemporaries emit cascades of vocalization with the flavor of human oratory, but that, alas, make no sense. The technical term—and the slang one, too—is "babbling," derived from the Biblical Tower of Babel, where there was plenty of sound but no comprehension. Sarah will keep babbling night and day—you'll hear her in her crib at night, spewing vowels and consonants. Not that she will be alone. Babies across cultures begin babbling at almost precisely the same age.

Nurseries in the United Kingdom, France, Japan, and Germany echo with sounds of babbling babies. In fact, even profoundly deaf children babble, although they have never heard oral speech. They babble first vocally, but when there is no feedback, they give up vocal babble. They then "babble" with their hands as if in adult sign language.

Baby Fact:

Babies acquire the ability to vocalize at different rates. For example, about 10 percent of babies start cooing during their first month, while another 10 percent don't start until nearly three months. Developmentally speaking, all of these babies are normal.

BEHIND THE SIGNS

Proud Papa

According to scientists studying the origins of human language, the first word to be uttered by Stone Age babies was quite likely "papa." Researchers believe the word may have been passed down through the generations from a "proto-language" spoken by all humans 50,000 years ago. However, other respected linguists argue that "papa," "dada," and "mama" are common terms in many cultures simply because they are the first babbled sounds made by babies. In fact, the word "papa" is used in almost 700 out of 1,000 world languages, and in 71 percent of cases it refers to either "father" or to a male relative on the father's side.

Babbling is a form of rehearsal for later speech. Like many other stages in child development, it springs from anatomical and neurological changes. A newborn's oral cavity—her "voice box"—is broad and short, and the sounds that come out of it are gurgles and snaffles. Gradually it lengthens and narrows, permitting more thrust and control of the upward puffs of air propelled across the vocal cords. Lips, tongue, and facial muscles are maturing too, facilitating sound formation. Meanwhile the baby is beginning to recognize vocalization as the way those "like me" reach out to one another, and she tries to mimic them.

Apart from the vowel sounds "eee" and "ooo," the first sounds produced by Baby are consonants like *b, d, m, n, w,* and *j*. That's because they are formed with the lips and tip of the tongue, familiar to babies from their well-known sucking motion, and strengthened from practice. Babies tend to string them together in long formations—"babababa" and "dadadadada." The babble has no meaning, not even to the baby, and is likely to be punctuated by abrupt changes in volume and pitch. Baby experiments with different pitches and intonations, and learns how to shout and whisper. Repetitive babbling then gives way to variegated babbling,

Baby Fact:

According to the experts, the average baby will utter a "real" word that has meaning for the first time anywhere between ten and fourteen months. However, the age range that is considered developmentally normal for this milestone is considerably wider.

her sounds or pretend to understand them; respond, rather, just to provide feedback and to let her know she's on the right communication track. Babbling babies with adult models who regularly talk back to them generally talk earlier than their peers and tend to use more words. Babies who receive little feedback are verbally slower and may even revert to earlier stages of development.

in which different syllables are mixed together in different ways—"badutigah" or "manmeba." And occasionally, a recognizable "real" word will be tossed in. Or at least so the parents believe.

Although the babbling is wordless, Baby mimics the way an adult would talk. Her vocalizations rise and fall like they do in adult speech, and she will pause after a torrent of syllables to await a response from her listener. In fact, she is likely to look squarely at the listener to make clear that a response is expected. Sometimes the string of syllables will have a rising inflection at the end, as though she were asking a question. By a year old, Baby knows thirty distinct sounds. She can reproduce all the vowel sounds and about half of the consonants, which is why she may say "fink" for "think" or "bwankie" for "blankie." It is particularly important at this stage to talk back to the baby. It's not necessary to repeat

WHAT'S THE POINT?

BABY EXPRESSES THOUGHTS BY POINTING

WHAT BABY DOES
Stretches out an arm and extends the forefinger.

WHAT BABY MEANS
'Look at that toy/dog/cake/balloon...'

WHAT YOU SHOULD NOTICE
Baby is making her first real 'statements'.

Nine-month-old Julie is in her high chair, picking up broken bits of cracker one by one and crunching them between her six brand-new teeth. Then, just outside the kitchen window, a white truck drives up. Distracted and excited, Julie drops the cracker bits and enthusiastically stabs a chubby finger toward the daily postal delivery. 'Look!' the pointing finger, accompanied by a torrent of babble, exclaims. 'It's the postman! My friend the postman!'

Everybody Gestures, One Way Or Another

Pointing as a form of communication is found in most cultures, but not always using the index-finger. Filipinos, for example, are likely to point with their chins, extending their necks and thrusting chins outward and upward to give directions. Children in the Australian outback point with the middle finger. People also 'point' by moving their eyes, heads, elbows or even feet. Researchers in Italy recorded six different forms of pointing, including with the index finger and with the whole hand. In many cultures, people point with the lips. Certain tribesmen in Ghana extend one or both lips to indicate direction.

Pointing is the infant's primary communication tool in the early months of life. It's an all-purpose tool, too. Well before speech and often along with babble, it expresses all manner of wants, interests, intriguing sights, expectations, friendship and curiosity. The pointing finger encompasses all of them. It is Julie's way of connecting to and acknowledging the world beyond herself. The extended finger – with its message of 'See what I see?' or 'Here's what I'm thinking' – will rapidly become the mainstay of her 'vocabulary' and her most used form of secret language. That dramatic point is a social tool, too. The finger says to those around her, 'Do you see what I see?'

The pointing finger also represents a signal advance in an infant's communicative development. For the first time, communication becomes a three-pronged affair, involving Julie, her 'listener' and the object or person they are communicating about. Scientists call it a 'triad'. Whereas Julie and her mother from birth were bound together by (scientifically speaking)

DO CHIMPANZEES POINT?

Yes, chimpanzees do point, according to one group of researchers, who have videotapes of the primates pointing at objects. Chimps are clearly seen extending their index fingers in the direction of desired food. It's a 'give me that' message – an obvious example of imperative pointing. Clint, a fourteen-year-old chimp, was seen repeatedly gesturing toward a bit of food that had fallen to the ground and then visually checking with the trainer to see if the trainer got the message.

One should note, however, that Clint and other apparent communicators are chimps in captivity, who have been trained and encouraged to point and rewarded when they do. And they point only to make requests of their trainers; no one has seen them pointing among themselves, seeking to call the attention of their fellow chimps to some mutually interesting object. Even to captive chimps, pointing does not seem to come naturally, and they are slow to interpret the meaning of pointing by others. In one experiment, researchers repeatedly pointed to the location of a hidden treat, but it took many trials for the chimps to locate it, and it was never certain that they had not just perhaps stumbled on it by trial and error.

Chimps in the wild, by all accounts, do not point. In one review of 600 hours of film of an African chimp colony, the scientists found only twenty-one instances in which chimps might be construed as finger-pointing to draw attention to a specific target. The consensus is that chimps do not point in the deliberate way human children do. Pointing as a communication tool is widely considered an ability unique to humans, like human speech. That being said, studies of chimp pointing continue, and the issue is not completely resolved.

intersubjectivity, now they have moved on to an additional stage called secondary intersubjectivity, meaning that other things and people are incorporated into their sphere of contemplation. Henceforth, Julie will be communicating about matters outside herself – the postman, the fire truck, the teddy bear – as well as her own needs. It is the beginning of adult communication and indeed comprises the very nature of communication itself. What do adults talk about if not other things and people besides themselves?

Infants all over the world begin pointing at around nine months of age, after they're able to sit firmly upright and take notice of the fascinating world around them. Cho-lin in Beijing will point to a toy or Grandmother at roughly the same developmental age as Lars in Stockholm or Cecelia in the

Philippines. Even deaf children begin pointing around the same time.

According to the late George Butterworth of the University of Sussex in England, whose lifetime research focused on the link between gesture and language, the ability to point with a purpose is innate in humans. Like the development of speech, it is a skill that sets us apart from other animals. Indeed, some ultrasound imagery seems to show forefinger extension by fetuses in the womb. Scientists in the UK have videotaped infants as early as two weeks using the forefinger independently. The finger extends in a straight position while the others curl into a kind of fist. Whether this actually qualifies as pointing is disputed, and it may simply reflect the infant's fascinating discovery of his own hands. By five months, a baby engages in a kind of rudimentary pointing as he reaches for objects and by eight to nine months, his finger definitely begins to train on an object or person.

'Declarative pointing' is the term researchers use. Julie's little forefinger is making a statement: 'That's my friend the postman!' or 'That's my clown doll!' Or, sometimes, arm crooked, she'll hold up the toy truck or coloured block to be admired. 'See, Mum?' Pointing also demands an audience, someone with whom to share the excitement of discovery, and is the little girl's way of incorporating a social circle. Babies never point when they're alone, according to those scientific videotapers snooping in on their every move. What's the sense in pointing out a wonderful sight when there's no one else around to notice it? With a pointing gesture, the child wants to engage someone in communication about what she's seen. The audience, though, need not necessarily be adult. Infants often point for the benefit of other children. Twins consistently point for each other, without regard to an adult audience.

Declarative pointing is a huge step forward in vocabulary development for you and your infant and begins to make her language a little less 'secret'. When she (or you) points at the family pet, you say, 'doggie'. Or when that motorised bird in the sky attracts her attention overhead, you come right back with, 'aeroplane'. When Julie points to an attractive toy beyond her reach or outside her playpen, you hold up the toy and say, 'Oh. You want the block?' Or, more creatively, you 'misunderstand' the message. 'You want the teddy bear?' holding it up. Firm shake of head in denial. 'Oh, the music box?' Another frustrated denial. 'How about the block?' A beaming smile signifies triumph! She has earned that desired block and has learned two more words besides.

Baby Fact:

Girls, on average, say their first word three weeks earlier than boys, and they learn pointing as a communication tool earlier, too.

ANOTHER POINTED MESSAGE

BABY MAKES REQUESTS AND DEMANDS BY POINTING

WHAT BABY DOES
Extends the arm and forefinger, and squeals.

WHAT BABY MEANS
'Bring me that!'

WHAT YOU SHOULD NOTICE
*Baby is expressing his first real requests,
demands or both.*

One day nine-month-old Jason, by now an experienced pointer, unveils a new trick. The forefinger jabs out in the same old fashion toward a fascinating object. But this time Jason isn't merely expressing interest or curiosity, or demonstrating his keen observation skills. He squeals and points, and you, his 'identifier', dutifully pick up what seems to be the target of the finger and say, 'Yes, that's your brother's football'. Jason still squeals and points, bouncing for emphasis. Puzzled, you pick it up again and say, 'ball'. Jason yelps in impatient protest, now wigwagging and semaphoring with his arms.

Now, instead of being merely an onlooker of his environment, he can manage, even manipulate, the people and things around him. When he was merely making statements about the ball or teddy bear, you might sometimes bring it to him. Now he understands that he can make that happen every time, using finger pointing, eye contact and some gurgles. When he wants something, he can 'ask' with his finger, and he'll get results. Of course, one of the shortcomings of pointing as a communicative gesture is that it's not specific. The pointing finger doesn't indicate precisely *what* the baby wants, only *where* it's located. Then it's up to you to start guessing. 'Is it this that you want? How about that?' Baby may grow increasingly impatient waiting for you to finally make the right choice. Identifying the desired object isn't always a total answer, either. Baby's curiosity extends practically back to day one, and what he wants to know isn't always just the name of an object; often he wants to know how the object works. Some version of the basic question 'What's that?' is an early part of Baby's language in every country, according to linguistic scholars – but this same non-verbal question can also translate to 'What does it do?' What occurs, somewhere around the tenth or eleventh month of life, is the maturation of different parts of Jason's brain, and thus more intricate forms of behaviour enter his repertoire. Early on, most of Jason's brain activity is initiated in the motor cortex. That basic region sent messages to the arms and legs and other parts, triggering movements and other important actions. Not much thinking or planning, in the adult sense, was involved in his more or less involuntary activities. But with the development of the prefrontal lobes, the 'thinking' part of the brain, Jason has become capable of planning an action, influencing the reaction of others, anticipating a result, watching it unfold as expected, and then repeating it. His actions begin to have

He doesn't want to just see the football from across the room. He wants to grasp it, inspect it above and below, smell it and hold it right there in his chubby hands. Naming the object 'football' for him isn't enough any longer. He wants to know what the ball feels like and what it looks like up close. 'Bring it to me!' the insistent finger is saying. At last you understand and happily deliver the goods.

Jason has now advanced from 'declarative pointing', making statements, to what is called 'imperative pointing', or 'requestive pointing'. 'Imperative pointing' is an important milestone in his development and, indeed, in his individuality.

WAS IT ALL A MISTAKE?

One school of scientific thought holds that children's pointing arises by accident. It represents a kind of failure: At around four months, babies start to reach for and grasp objects. But sometimes their reach falls short or they're unable to grasp the object. An adult witnessing the failure interprets the outstretched arm as pointing at the object and hands it to the child. Therefore, afterward the child only gestures toward an object and succeeds in receiving it.

the ring of purposefulness, and he now does many things intentionally rather than by reflex or habit. Jason is definitely more than a spectator now: he's a player.

Being able to communicate the message 'bring me that', implies another important advance in Jason's life. He now has a fully-fledged memory. Parents, say, of a one- or two-year-old may make a statement like, 'We took him to see the Queen's birthday procession and he liked the horses and the carriage. Too bad he won't remember any of it when he grows up'. A remark such as this confuses two important processes in human development. 'Recall' refers to the ability to reach back into the brain's storehouse of past events and recreate it in the mind's eye. 'Memory', however, is at the heart of learning and of life itself. We are unconsciously remembering, putting memories into practice, with everything we do. Even automatic behaviour, like walking or dancing, is based on what we learned earlier and now call to mind without going through an obvious brow-furrowing thought process. We operate on automatic pilot. Jason extends the finger

To Point or Not To Point?

American and European children are taught early that it is rude to point at people, but okay to point to indicate directions. Among Navajos, pointing with an extended finger is strictly taboo, but it is permissible to point with the hand as long as all fingers are extended. Pointing with a motion of the elbow is permissible, too. In some African cultures, pointing with the right hand is approved, but pointing with the left hand is considered insulting.

of imperative pointing because he has learned that it will bring results. That thought and the corresponding action is embedded in his memory, to be called forward and practised as needed.

As Jason begins imperative pointing to get what he wants, he'll develop other forms of secret language, too. He'll hold out his arm and wiggle curled fingers toward himself in the classic 'come here' gesture. He may signal that he's hungry by bringing his hands to his mouth. Gazing out of the window, he may flap his arms to demonstrate that he's seen a bird. Always, of course, he'll look at your eyes to make sure you received the message. Return with an understanding look, and try to verbalise for him the message you think he may be sending ('You want Daddy to come over?' 'Is Jason hungry?' 'Did Jason see a bird?') to reassure him that he is understood and also to provide the early building blocks for his future verbal communication skills.

Baby Fact:

Research has shown that gestures such as pointing are especially helpful to baby boys, who are often later verbal communicators and may need to alleviate physical frustration and stress.

NOW YOU GET THE POINT

A POINTED CONVERSATION

WHAT BABY DOES
*Stretches the arm out and extends the forefinger
after you pose a simple question. ('Where's Fido?')*

WHAT BABY MEANS
'Look. There's what you asked me about.'

WHAT YOU SHOULD NOTICE
*Baby is answering your simple questions,
thus the beginning of real 'conversation'.*

S andra, a few days shy of a year old, sits in her high chair at the family dining table. She's gurgling, smiling and pointing. She hasn't spoken her first understandable word yet, although she certainly babbles. Nonetheless, she's aware of everyone and everything around her and even seems to be following the bob and weave of the conversation. 'Where's Daddy?' you ask. Instantly a chubby finger levels itself at the beaming adult male across the table. Wow! 'Where's the doggie?' Downward points the finger at the wagging tail of the little terrier under her chair. Guess what? Sandra is making conversation!

By now Sandra seems to understand forty to fifty spoken words – words like 'bottle', 'bed', 'car', 'blanket' and 'bye bye'. Understanding the link between the spoken word and her responsive gesture is something new and a critical step in her development. Now she clearly fathoms the central and important role of language: Spoken words refer to seen objects, people, actions, even feelings. You may ask her if she's hungry and she'll motion toward her high chair. She'll look in that direction, maybe even crawl toward it.

She's even progressed a step beyond that. If you mention Daddy before he appears, she may point toward the empty chair where Daddy usually sits.

Baby Fact:

Studies have shown that a one-year-old can reproduce the word for an object within a week after pointing to it.

Little Ladies First

By fourteen months, the average boy baby can say five individual words. The average girl's spoken vocabulary is almost four times as large. By sixteen months, the average number of words a child understands is 169, although some, mostly girls, may understand as many as 400.

If you ask about an aeroplane, she may point skyward, whether or not there's an aircraft overhead. She clearly understands that words stand for objects or people whether they're present or not. Her auditory and visual senses are now working together. She links what she sees with the spoken words she hears.

Somewhere in the days or weeks leading up to that key moment Sandra has attained what the child-development researcher Michael Tomasello of the Max Planck Institute in Germany has termed 'joint attention'. Joint attention occurs when you and your infant focus on the same object or action at the same time, but also recognise the existence of

EVERYBODY'S DOING IT

Pointing and signaling seems to be built into the human constitution. In a unique study, Susan Goldin-Meadow of the University of Chicago looked at four profoundly deaf children whose parents had normal hearing. The parents had deliberately not exposed their children to American Sign Language or their own hand signals because they wanted the children to enroll in a programme that would help them develop normal oral speech.

Nonetheless, the children began pointing and gesturing at seven months, like hearing children, and gradually developed their own system of sign language and communication. They even worked out their own grammar to make themselves clear and developed signals that indicated pronouns or plurals. Goldin-Meadow later found the same kind of signaling among deaf Taiwanese children and has begun studying deaf children in Spain and Turkey.

Too far for pointing?

Infants' pointing may be limited by their nearsightedness. Studies have shown that infants first begin to point at objects at close visual range and gradually at those farther away, but typically are not able to discern objects at greater distance until full adult vision arrives at about one year of age. The dog in the neighbour's yard or the tree across the street may be too blurred for them to see clearly and thus gain their attention. They may very well not be able to follow an adult's effort to direct them toward a plane overhead or a car or building on the horizon.

that mutual attention. Several developmental steps occur before that happens. At nine months, Sandra can point or gesture toward objects she sees or wants. But when *you* point to the object, her eyes at this age do not follow the direction of the point. More likely, they will train on the end of your pointing finger. Nor does she follow the direction of your eyes as they seek out the desired object. And when she herself points at the cuddly teddy bear, she hasn't learned to look at your face to make sure you've received the message.

It is typically not until her first birthday that all these fragments click into a single equation. Mastering eye contact comes first. Sandra learns (by trial and error) that she must have your attention if her quest for dinner or the teddy bear is to be successful, and that the way to get that critical attention is to look you squarely in the eye. Even wigwagging with her arms or saying 'uh-uh-uh' isn't enough. Now you're on the same wavelength and she can see your eyes are zeroing in on the same object. She now understands that it's not the finger she should be looking at, but its direction. And then comes

the 'Where's Daddy?' moment we looked at earlier, when she begins to make the association between the word and the object.

The late George Butterworth of the University of Sussex has called the co-ordination of words and hand signals the foundational building block of human communication. For the first time Sandra realises that a specific word designates a specific object or person; when Mum uses the word 'doggie', she means the amiable household pet, even if Fido is nowhere in sight. Sandra's initial understood vocabulary will be mostly single words, usually nouns for things or people. But soon she'll move on to words for actions ('eat', 'walk') and feelings ('Sleepy, Sandra?').

Of course, you've been teaching her for months, perhaps without realising it. When you say 'Daddy' or 'doggie', perhaps glancing or pointing, neural connections occur in the prefrontal cortex, and each time you repeat the word and gesture, the connection is strengthened. Gradually associating 'Daddy' with that genial man across the table becomes automatic. The lesson becomes especially vivid if you emphasise the identifying word ('There's the *doggie*!' 'There's *Daddy*!') so don't be shy about playing it up!

Still Get The Point?

As vocabulary grows, pointing will become a less important way for Sandra to communicate but will by no means disappear. Pointing and gesturing play key roles in cultures and languages the world over, even though the exact details of the gesture differ. Susan Goldin-Meadow, at the University of Chicago, has shown that pointing and gesturing are central to communication even in the absence of speech. Working with four siblings, all of whom were completely deaf, Goldin-Meadow found that they had worked out an entire vocabulary of signs, signals and gestures all their own and communicated in that language even after they had learned American Sign Language.

HANDS UP!

BABY WANTS OUT AND NEEDS YOUR HELP

WHAT BABY DOES
Stretches both arms upward.

WHAT BABY MEANS
'Get me out of here!'

WHAT YOU SHOULD NOTICE
*Baby is simultaneously demonstrating his independence
(I want my freedom) and dependence (I need your help
to get me out).*

Peter's arms are raised in the air, pointing straight at the heavens. There's an imploring, please-help-me look on his face, alternating with an expression of anticipation. You might compare his gesturing posture to an athlete crossing the finish line in triumph. There's even a 'Hail, Caesar!' quality to it.

But Peter's message is quite different. In one form of this multipurpose gesture, he's saying he's had enough of his present location and wants a change of venue. 'I'm finished pushing these crackers around. Get me out of this boring high chair.' And up go the pleading arms, unmistakably asking to be snatched up and removed from his present confinement. Or his message might also be, 'That loud noise scared me. Please pick me up and show me there's nothing to be afraid of'. Or, Peter, in his cot with arms overhead, might be saying 'I've slept long enough. Take me out to where the action is'.

This bit of 'secret' language is hardly a secret. The caregiver may confront it beseechingly several times a day and must fashion a response on the context. Part of it is a form of parent-child interaction, based on hugs and holding and being close together. It also conveys a mixed message. Baby wants out of jail and wants his independence. At the same time, he recognises that he's dependent on you to grant him his freedom.

'Carry You!'

When toddlers begin to talk and put words together, they quickly learn their own names plus mother and father. Pronouns, however, are a little trickier. 'You' and 'me' and 'I' are confusing: Sometimes I'm 'me', sometimes Mum calls me 'you' and sometimes Mum is 'you'. A common confusion occurs when a tired baby holds up his arms to Daddy and implores 'Carry you!' Of course, he's not offering to pick up Dad, just looking for a welcome lift.

Sometimes Peter's upstretched arms can become part of an interactive game, a game taught by the parent, Grandpa or a doting uncle. 'How big is Baby? So big!' And Daddy, Grandpa or Uncle Joe thrusts his arms up in the air, to show Baby's supposed growth to a giant size. Peter, a natural copycat, hears the words, sees the upraised arms and imitates Daddy's, Grandpa's or Uncle Joe's exuberant upward motions with his own little arms. Soon, just the words, 'How big is Baby?'

will start the upward motion, just as in Pavlov's famous conditioned-response experiment with dogs. Sometimes, though, Peter may raise his arms without the cue, simply in an effort to get the attention getting game going.

This game is an example of Baby observing, learning, translating his observations into body language, and using that language to get results. Indeed, it's one of the first lessons. As soon as a four-month-old

🛒 Baby Fact:

Babies tend to focus on one skill at a time as they are learning. For instance, while a child is intent upon mastering the skill of pulling up, she will be less likely to babble or practise her hand gestures. With infant development, it's mainly one thing at a time.

can control the movements of his arms and make the association between the arm motion and being soothingly picked up, the lesson has been initiated. It is a lesson firmly in place by the time Baby is sitting without support but still can't get around for himself, and it may continue even when Baby is mobile and can stand alone. Up go the arms to be lifted out of the playpen or the cot. The language often persists into the toddler and preschool age, when Baby is tired and wants to be picked up and carried, rather than being forced to walk.

YOU GOT MY BACK?

HOW AND WHY MOBILE BABIES SEEK REASSURANCE

WHAT BABY DOES
Crawls quickly away from you,
but continually glances back.

WHAT BABY MEANS
"Are you still there? Is this okay with you?

WHAT YOU SHOULD NOTICE
Baby, although independent, still needs
your presence and support.

ashley is mobile. After months of having to rely on you to get her from place to place, she can now scoot and scramble on all fours. She can happily navigate across the living room, even pull herself to a standing position on the furniture. (Not so happily for you, she can now also reach for precious fragile objects or head for that forbidden spot by the hearth.) Set her down and away she goes as fast as hands and knees will propel her. Nothing stops her from moving about; however, every ten feet or so, she'll interrupt her forward progress and glance back warily over her shoulder, with a look that is sometimes apprehensive, sometimes mischievous.

"Mom, are you still there?" is one message that glance sends. The other is: "Mom, aren't you going to stop me?" At nine months, Ashley feels the first twinges of separation anxiety, that state of mild fearfulness about the possible absence of Mom, the person to whom she has been so tenaciously and emotionally attached, the guardian of her welfare. Mom may be only a few steps or scrambles away, still within earshot, but Ashley needs the reassurance that she's not out of sight. After all, Mom is her main source of food, dry diapers, and loving oohs and coos. The fear of being apart from her will go on from here and perhaps become more marked as the months advance, especially when it becomes time to be separated for day care or a neighborhood play group.

Baby Fact:

Once your little one is crawling, it is time to baby-proof your home. Get down on your hands and knees, cruise around, try to imagine all the hazards Baby might come in contact with, and get rid of them!

Hanging in There

The tension between clinging to Mom and reaching out for new experiences has been compared to dangling from a tree limb. You don't want to let go of the limb until your feet safely touch the ground.

"Mom, aren't you going to stop me?" is another side of the same coin. A nine-month-old like Ashley is boundlessly curious, especially about all those interesting things that until now have been beyond her reach. She'll head for temptation at the first scuttling opportunity. At the same time she knows—or will learn quickly from your wagging finger, shaking head, or forceful "No, Ashley!"—that some things are definitely off-limits. Prohibition, of course, may only enhance the attractiveness of these things. So she may well zero in on that vulnerable antique vase, recognizing both that it's a no-no and that her destination is bound to get your attention. Hence the over-the-shoulder glance to see if you are coming, combined with a request for intervention. When she is finally scooped up and out of the way (or the vase is moved to safer surroundings), Ashley may actually emit a mischievous little giggle.

THE NINE-MONTH REVOLUTION

The twin tugs of attachment to Mom and curiosity about the world are central events in what Philippe Rochat of Emory University in Atlanta, Georgia, has called the Nine-Month Revolution. Like the Two-Month Revolution, it signifies a marked and important change in Baby's life and behavior. Increasingly he reaches beyond himself and incorporates the outside world into his life: He points to things that interest him, "asks questions" about objects, and becomes sensitive to the emotions of others. He wants to know, and he wants to experience. And as he becomes more and more mobile, he has the capacity to experience and explore and, most of all, to gain the reactions and input of others. At the same time, novelty can be a little scary, and unfamiliar people and unfamiliar objects frightening. His caregiver is his safe haven. So he simultaneously clings and reaches out.

This revolution has an anatomical basis. The prefrontal lobes of the brain are the slowest to develop, and these areas control such things as memory, attention, planning, inhibition, and others. But between nine and twelve months there is a spurt of development in the prefrontal lobes. Previously, both Baby's memory and attention span were short; he didn't point to interesting objects because they didn't hold his attention for that long. He couldn't mentally devise a plan like, "That's a tempting vase over there. If I just reach out my arm far enough I can grab it." His attachment to Mom evolves in a similar way. It's hard to maintain a full attachment when your short-term memory is measured in a few seconds. But at nine months, with burgeoning prefrontal lobes, his memory dramatically increases, and he can hold tight to Mom and her attachment. He doesn't want to let go of her. He sees another, unfamiliar face as a threat to that attachment. At the same time, his curiosity and his I-see-it-I-want-it-I-can-figure-how-to get-it skills are expanding, too. For Baby, the nine-month revolution is both an opportunity and a time of conflict.

The backward glance for reassurance signifies another developmental milestone in Ashley's growth. Separation anxiety demonstrates her innate unwavering attachment to her mother—a characteristic that the little human shares with infants of many other species. John Bowlby of London's famous Tavistock Clinic pointed out this phenomenon in a 1949 scientific article that upended conventional wisdom about children's physical and emotional growth. Until then, it was firmly believed that a child bonded to her mother in infancy simply to fulfill needs; babies would attach themselves to anyone who unfailingly fed, cleansed, or swaddled them, and good mothering

from any kind woman (or man) was enough to forge the bond. Freud's daughter Anna championed that view. She called it "cupboard love."

Bowlby said that mother-infant bonding existed from birth, pointing to parallels in other animals. When baby ducklings or goslings hatch, they follow the first moving creature they see (whether it's a mother goose or passing human, as the film *Fly Away Home* demonstrated vividly) and this attachment continues until maturity. Then in 1958 psychologist Harry Harlow at the University of Wisconsin modified the theories about the origins of motherly love. In his experiment, baby monkeys adopted a warm, terry-cloth-covered surrogate mother fashioned of wire mesh and rigged with a nipple and milk supply, preferring "her" even though another apparatus also offered a sucking nipple and adequate nutrition but little comfort. This showed that babies made their caring bond not only with something that provides for them, but also with something that is cozy and nice to hug.

When the backward glance translates as "Is this okay, Mom?" it represents a different step in Ashley's development. Now the developing brain can process the concept that some things are approved and some things forbidden. "That vase is so pretty, but Mom might not like it if I touch it." Curiosity comes into conflict with the need for Ashley to maintain her mother's approval.

Overcoming separation anxiety—or stranger anxiety, which often accompanies it—can be a slow, even painful process. There are practical ways to help your child overcome these fears, although simply providing a safe and protective environment will encourage your baby in his journey towards greater independence.

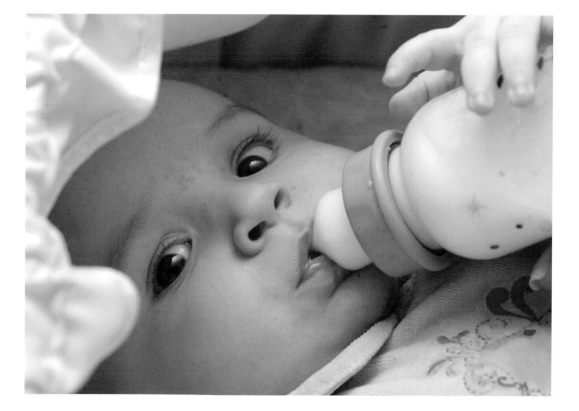

WHO IS THAT GUY?

DETECTING BABY'S FIRST BIT OF STRANGER ANXIETY

WHAT BABY DOES

*Clings to you and cries at the approach
of a strange adult.*

WHAT BABY MEANS

*"I don't feel comfortable around this person.
Get me away from him!"*

WHAT YOU SHOULD NOTICE

New faces and new experiences can be scary.

Baby Nguyen has always been super-friendly. When he was six months old he bestowed winning smiles on all the shoppers at the supermarket and giggled when a grandmotherly stranger tickled him under the chin. But now Nguyen is nine months old. Those admiring overtures from people outside the immediate family circle are rejected with horror—even from his Grandma, who simply adores him. Let an unfamiliar face appear and he clings, whines, and looks terrified. The message of his body language is unmistakable: "Get that person out of here!" No problem figuring it out.

"Stranger anxiety" is the technical term for Nguyen's unhappy actions. You'll see it to a greater or lesser degree for the next months or even years. As with separation anxiety as discussed in the previous chapter, stranger anxiety results from a combination of changes rushing over Nguyen in the last three months of the first year of life. He is feeling simultaneously the strong ties of attachment to Mom and the powerful impulse to reach out and explore new worlds. The "thinking" areas of the brain are maturing along with those devoted to long-term memory. The face of his main caregiver is the face he remembers well; these newcomers are just fleeting faces. Indeed, in his mind, they may even be threats.

BEHIND THE SIGNS

Sneaking Away

Should you always say "bye bye" to a clingy baby? Experts feel that giving an anxious baby notice of your departure is preferable to sneaking out when he is occupied with the baby-sitter. Although you may achieve temporary success and a "clean break" the first time, too many unannounced exits can ultimately result in excessive clinginess when you return home and in future situations. Your child may come to fear that you could disappear without warning at any time.

Nguyen may balk at unfamiliar places, too. Shepherd him to the playground and he may hang back from the slide he enjoyed at six months old. It has vanished in the mists of his short-term memory. He may have a problem with baby-sitters, child-care providers, or his first play group, where he'll stay on your lap, perhaps sucking his thumb and shielding his eyes from the others. (And, he may not be alone! The play group may well consist of four one-year-olds sitting on their mothers' laps, industriously pulling on their thumbs and expressing their woes in the same baby body language.)

Smart Kids

Children often recognize separation problems as readily as parents do. Once the author came to stay with two-year-old Lucy and her father while Lucy's mother was called away, far from home, for a few days because of a family emergency. Grandpa Ed and Lucy had an ongoing close relationship based on "reading" books together, and he had stayed with Lucy several times before. But the moment Lucy's mother departed, the little girl set up a howl, refused to approach Grandpa Ed, threw away books when they were offered to her, and clung anxiously to her father. Clearly she realized this was no short-term separation, and she did not smile or open books until her mother returned.

So, what's a mother to do? The first step is to anticipate. An inevitable phase of separation anxiety is to be expected sooner or later, so do some groundwork to minimize it. One important strategy is to start short-term separation early on, certainly within six months. (Remember that an evening out is good therapy for parents, too.) Bring the sitter in early so he or she becomes friendly with your child. If possible, schedule the same sitter for future dates. At play group, stay with your child for the entire visit and remain within eyesight when you set him down. You will find him checking on you frequently; reassure him by your physical presence. Introduce him slowly to full-time child care.

Baby Fact:

Babies often surprise their parents by becoming suddenly fearful of new people as they approach the end of their first year—even babies who have previously been extremely "sociable" and happy around strangers.

YOUR LITTLE COPYCAT

THE IMPORTANCE OF IMITATIVE LEARNING

WHAT BABY DOES
Imitates your actions as she plays.

WHAT BABY MEANS
"I want to be like Mom and Dad."

WHAT YOU SHOULD NOTICE
You are Baby's constant role model.

Ten-month-old Rachel is sitting in your living room, which is littered with her toys. She picks them up one by one, examines them, and puts them down. She looks at the stuffed dog, squeezes him, and babbles. Then her eyes settle on a yellow rattle shaped like a banana. She shakes it, listens, and then holds one end to her ear and the other near her mouth. She babbles. Rachel is carrying on a telephone conversation, just like you do.

Isn't that funny? You can't help but smile. But Rachel's endearing impersonation represents something more significant than just a cute performance. She is rehearsing a behavior that will become the cornerstone of her secret language—one that will play a key role in her ongoing development from here on in. Early on, even from the first hours after birth, she has recognized that others are "like me." And she wants to duplicate your actions, to be "like you." At first she merely observed and absorbed. Now her new mobility, growing independence, and burgeoning motor skills allow her to review what she has seen—and imitate it.

If imitation is the sincerest form of flattery, babies are the greatest flatterers of all. They imitate your actions from morning to night. Virtually every gesture in Rachel's secret language is patterned after your behavior, sometimes without your being aware of it.

Baby Fact:

Studies show that babies prefer to imitate other children rather than adults.

That shake of the head for "no" or nod for "yes" is an early lesson from you. The pointing index finger is a gesture you've used many times. Indeed, profiling deaf children who had invented their own sign

Say "aaaaa"

Lift your newborn from the crib and confront him en face. When you make eye contact, blink and watch to see if he blinks, too. Then stick out your tongue as if a doctor were examining your throat. Hold it there. Baby will probably stick out his tongue, too, when he sees your tongue. Babies don't always respond instantly. You may see him moving his tongue inside his mouth, as if testing which body part to use. One six-week-old waited a whole day before his tongue came out.

language, Susan Goldin-Meadow found that they too used common adult hand communications like thumbs-up for okay and an upraised palm for "No more, thank you."

The critical importance of imitation in Baby's development has become more fully understood only in recent decades. The child-study pioneer Jean Piaget believed babies could not imitate until they were several months old. In 1977, Andrew Meltzoff, then at Oxford University in England, conducted a simple but revolutionary experiment. He simply stuck out his tongue at twelve babies sixteen to twenty-one days old and watched in fascination as they mirrored his behavior, sticking out their tongues in response. Yet the babies had never seen their own faces, let alone their tongues. How could they possibly do that?

THIS JUST IN

An eleven-month-old will follow an adult's eye direction as he or she trains on an interesting object. "Hey, what you're looking at is fascinating!" Does gaze following help babies learn, by cluing them into what adults find worth looking at? And, specifically, as an early instance of secret language and a precursor of pointing, does it advance child development and the mastery of language?

Andrew Meltzoff and Rechele Brooks of the University of Washington decided to explore the link between gaze following and language development in a landmark study reported in the journal *Developmental Science*. Meltzoff and Brooks looked at ninety-six infants aged nine, ten, and eleven months, half of them male and half of them female.

In the university lab, infants sat on their mothers' laps facing an experimenter. After gaining the child's attention with toys, the experimenter made eye contact and then turned her head and eyes to the side. In some cases the experimenter closed her eyes before she turned her head. In others they remained open. She repeated the head-turn four times. Two synchronized video cameras recorded both the child's face and the experimenter's.

Nine-month-olds followed the adult's head turn whether her eyes were open or not. A majority of eleven- and twelve-month-olds followed the adult only when her eyes were open and she seemed clearly to be looking at an object. They did not follow when her eyes were closed. And they also "talked" with "uh-uh" and "hmm" sounds, as though commenting on the experimenter's gaze. They clearly made a connection between the looker and the object and might have also been showing a psychological sharing of common interest.

When the children were eighteen months old, they were tested on a standard measure of language ability. Those who scored highest in following adult open-eye gaze scored far higher in word comprehension. They understood nearly twice as many words, on average, as did the others. They knew the meanings of 337 words. In speaking, however, their scores were lower—194 words—and roughly equal to those of the closed-eye group. Meltzoff and Brooks concluded that word production depends on the development of other skills, like strength of tongue and lips and development of the vocal cords. Nevertheless, gaze following was identified as a key building block in development of children's language.

Although the report by Meltzoff and M. Keith Moore of the University of Washington in Seattle was initially greeted with skepticism, since then infant tongue protrusion studies have been replicated dozens of times in laboratories around the world. Younger and younger babies have been shown to imitate tongue protrusion, including one a mere forty-two minutes old. They imitate other facial expressions, too. They will open their mouths wide, blink their eyes, or pout with their lips if they see an adult do it. Babies, it seems, are natural copycats. Mom and Dad are their everpresent role models.

Seven Wonders

Infants younger than two months have been observed imitating seven types of adult movements when prompted:

- **Mouth opening**

- **Hand movements**

- **Emotional facial expressions**

- **Head movements**

- **Lip protrusion and cheek movements**

- **Eye blinking**

- **Tongue protrusion**

Does your baby arrive with ability to imitate on day one? One group of researchers thinks so. Just as humans may be pre-programmed to develop speech, infants may come equipped with a capacity to study others' actions and reproduce them themselves. Furthermore, just as humans are the only species gifted with speech, they are believed to be the only ones able to imitate. Contrary to popular perception, a primate's ability to imitate isn't quite the same as ours. Monkeys can be taught, but they can't spontaneously imitate other monkeys simply by watching. Older chimps in the wild have been seen "teaching" younger animals to crack nuts by hammering them between stones, but there is no evidence they can reproduce actions they've seen before, as Rachel did with her banana telephone.

Baby Fact:

Researchers have noticed that in twins, one sibling tends to consistently be the "doer" or "practicer" while the other sibling is the thoughtful "observer." Once a feat is mastered by the former, the latter can immediately imitate the action successfully without having practiced at all.

ENOUGH ALREADY!

HOW BABY EXPRESSES FRUSTRATION AND OVERSTIMULATION

WHAT BABY DOES

*Opens her mouth, snorts, and signals "stop"
with her hands.*

WHAT BABY MEANS

"That's enough now."

WHAT YOU SHOULD NOTICE

*A sudden switch from a happy mood to an upset one
usually means Baby is overstimulated.*

Was that a yawn? But surely Colleen couldn't be sleepy. She has just had a nap, she has been fed, and she has been thoroughly enjoying herself the last few minutes. Her brother has been playing "I'm gonna get you," crawling across the floor, sending her scuttling ahead of him and cackling with glee. Her music box had been caroling, cartoon figures have been galloping across the TV, and you've been clapping your hands at the rambunctious floor show. A yawn? And that hand? Why is she holding up that hand?

Babies love a good time. They love to crawl, to be chased, and most of all to be the center of attention. Music and voices delight them. But sometimes, for a nine-month-old like Colleen, enough is enough. Too many stimuli coming too fast are more than a young growing brain can assimilate. Too many neurons are firing at once. Colleen sends out a signal: "Stop, stop. I need to withdraw." She stops crawling, plops down, and holds up her hand like a traffic cop. Her actions are telling you that she needs to be calmed down, and that if you don't come to the rescue she may burst into tears, and begin to tremble, and it may be a long stretch before Colleen is herself again.

Baby Fact:

Babies are like adults: they sometimes need a break from the action and occasionally have solitary moods.

BABY TESTS

If a newborn were to be held and his head was allowed to drop suddenly while his trunk was supported, he would throw out his arms and legs and then bring his arms together in a kind of embrace. This reaction is called the Moro reflex, and it's one test a doctor may use to ensure that the baby's reflexes are working properly. Another test is for the Babinski reflex. In this, a finger is drawn up the baby's sole from heel to toe, which prompts the big toe to flex, followed by a fanning out of the other toes. The reflex is normally present in children up to a year old, or until the child can bear weight on his feet.

Overstimulation is possibly the part of babies' secret language most difficult for a parent to interpret. One reason may be that its onset is often so unexpected, as in Colleen's case. One moment she is the life of the party and the next moment she is sending out an SOS. It's a mixed signal, too, combining messages from many directions with potentially different meanings. Is she yawning because she's sleepy? Whining because she's hungry? Burying her face because she feels shy? Pinning her arms to her sides because she's afraid? Holding up her hand because … well, why?

Despite its subtlety, the signal for overstimulation is an important one to notice. Ideally, you want to intervene before the uncomfortable moment transforms into genuine, full-blown distress and an outburst of crying.

On other side of the overstimulation coin, we find boredom. In older children, body language related to boredom is readily recognizable. They're the ones who fuss and act up when they're in a restaurant or being wheeled through a shopping mall where they can't see or touch anything. Infants show boredom with a kind of glassy-eyed stare, accompanied by whining, grunts, and flailing of the arms.

Babies need stimulation. They thrive on it. In fact, brain development depends on it. Indeed, lack of stimulation can have serious results, as in the famous case of the Romanian orphanage. Children there, receiving no adult attention or stimulation, actually showed reduced and delayed brain growth. But simply swamping a child with stimuli—toys, sounds, activities—isn't the answer, either. Restraint is important. Novelty is important, too. Introduce only a few new toys at a time to avoid overstimulation, and get in the habit of rotating Baby's playthings so that boredom doesn't set in.

BEHIND THE SIGNS

Rough-Housing

It's fun for Dad—and maybe for Baby, too. Rolling and romping around the living room floor, tickling and tackling, amid giggling and hilarity. Or snatching up Baby and hoisting her overhead, even tossing her in the air and catching her on the downward plunge. As Baby giggles, she expresses a combination of happiness and fear. It's an easy line to cross. Watch for tensed hands and widened, frightened eyes as signals to end the game. Better yet, it's best to end vigorous play before reaching this point and before exhaustion sets in, so err on the side of sooner rather than later.

COMMON CUES FOR OVERSTIMULATION

All babies express the message "enough" in their own particular way. It's important that you discover your child's special way of communicating feelings of overstimulation, and yet sometimes these are very hard to detect. Especially difficult is the very young infant whose repertoire of body language is still somewhat limited. To get you started, here are a few common gestures as suggested by Connie Marshall, R.N., author of *From Here to Maternity*, that often translate as "Okay, enough, knock it off now."

- Snoring
- Sneezing
- Yawning
- Hiccups
- Whimpering

- Sucking noises
- Bored expression
- Eyelids half closed
- Glassy stare
- Looking tired

- Wrinkled nose
- Raised upper lip
- Shutting the eyes
- Turning head away from you

If you don't pick up on the message and you continue with the undesired activity, your child will become further annoyed and might:

- Draw arms close to the torso and flail the hands about
- Hold the arms and legs straight and stiff   ■ Clasp the hands together
- Cry, wail, or have a full-on fit, depending on your level of persistence

TOYS ARE US

PLAYTHINGS THAT PROMOTE
BABY-PARENT COMMUNICATION

"*Brian, where is your doll?*" *you ask, and eleven-month-old Brian triumphantly—proudly—gestures toward the Teletubbie propped in a corner of his crib.* "*And where is your ball?*" *He obediently rolls it to you, or at least in your general direction.* "*Uh-uh-uh,*" *he says, pointing. The sounds and gesture are secret baby language for* "*Bring me my Paddington Bear.*"

Toys are among the first objects an infant can recognize and identify from spoken words. About half the words a one-year-old understands are words for objects, most of them toys. Thus much of Baby's secret language focuses on playthings— names for trucks, stuffed animals, and rattles, as well as phrases such as "Bring me this" and "I want to play with that."

The importance of toys in child development goes well beyond gesturing, pointing, and building passive vocabulary, however. Toys help a child understand his world, but they also promote the basic components of parent–child relationship— communication and interaction.

Every toy can be a prop for give-and-take between parent and child. Brian's ball, for instance, rolling across the playroom floor, promotes the idea of taking turns. First Mother rolls it, then Brian tries to roll it back. Most games that parents and babies play together involve just that kind of rhythmic dance, in which each partner performs certain choreographed steps, patiently waiting for the other to perform. Taking turns is what interpersonal relationships, and especially conversation, is all

about. Indeed, early in the baby's life, parent and child engage in "protoconversations," in which Mom talks to Baby, and then, when she finishes, Baby takes his conversational role by smiling, giggling, or windmilling with his arms.

Be aware that some toys promote interaction better than others. A toy for a preverbal child needs to be

"90 percent child and 10 percent toy," says Kathy Hirsh-Pasek, of Temple University, Philadelphia, a researcher in children's creativity. She recommends toys that a child can push, hug, "talk" to, pick up, or throw, or that can move or make noises, which is why rattles are a centuries-old, worldwide favorite. Other good choices are toys that can be held up and "commented" on via gestures and motions. Best of all are those playthings that can be passed back and forth, with suitable vocalizations and reactions, between infant and parent. Toys like these inspire creativity and exploration, even at an early age.

Quality playthings are not necessarily manufactured toys or items purchased at the shopping mall. A one-year-old's favorite game may be to cover his stuffed tiger with the crib blanket, say "all gone!" (a favorite early phrase) and then dramatically "discover" the missing jungle cat again with squeals of feigned surprise and delight. No fancy, expensive toys needed for that one! One psychologist recorded a child "hiding" and magically "finding" a toy fifteen consecutive times and squealing delightedly every time.

Here are some more suggestions for toys that will aid in developing your baby's secret language skills:

A MOBILE, of course, is an early favorite. It should have bright colors, intriguing shapes, and plenty of eyecatching motion. (Pastel-colored mobiles, although they may enhance your nursery's décor, will not hold as much interest for Baby.) Infants do become bored with the same old familiar objects, so the mobile should be changed periodically.

STUFFED ANIMALS to hold, hug, and talk to. They make perfect role-play partners for Baby when you are not around!

JACK-IN-THE-BOX. One-year-olds like surprises, real or imagined, even if they're a bit frightened at first when Jack pops out of his hiding place. See Baby quiver with expectancy while waiting for Jack to abruptly appear, and urge you again and again to wind Jack up. BOXES of different shapes and sizes that Baby can stuff objects into and retrieve. Stacking boxes is another favorite activity.

PUZZLES that you and Baby can solve together. Look for the ones with bright colors and large, chunky pieces. Praise Baby with appropriate comments: "You found the right piece! Good!" Name for him the objects depicted on the puzzle.

MUSICAL INSTRUMENTS. A xylophone, piano, or other percussion instrument will delight Baby as he pounds on it to make "musical" noises.

CLOTH OR HEAVY CARDBOARD PICTURE BOOKS whose pages can't be successfully eaten, torn, or thrown but that you and Baby can "read" together: "Find the piggie! There he is!"

A MUSIC BOX, preferably one that plays with a definite rhythm. Babies respond to rhythm, and one theory is that it traces to the womb, where Mother's heartbeat insistently dominated.

ARE WE HAVING FUN YET?

GAMES THAT PROMOTE BABY-PARENT INTERACTION

*P*lay is the child's work, the child-development pioneer Jean Piaget declared. By playing, children try out ideas and learn about themselves, their world, and those who populate it. And parent-child games are at the heart of this learning curve. Parent–child games foster communication and the idea of taking turns, and they help to perfect babies' secret language. Here are games that promote those goals—and are fun besides.

BIRTH TO SIX MONTHS

THE SOUND OF MUSIC

Give your baby an early musical treat by performing a "recital" of different sounds that come from different soundmakers. Start with your own voice. Put your baby on your lap facing you. Sing part of a well-known nursery rhyme. Brothers and sisters can add their own performances, too. Pause and smile with every phrase, just in case your baby is ready to join in.

Whistle short simple tunes, like "Rock-a-bye Baby," or whatever song your baby likes best. Not only will she appreciate the familiar tune, but soon she'll try to imitate your pursed lip.

Try playing a kazoo or harmonica or click on castanets. Soon your baby will be reaching for your musical instruments, so you can take turns or play a duet.

TICKLE, TICKLE

A lot of the laughs in tickling come from anticipating the pleasure. Try to have a regular time, such as after Baby's bath, for the game. Vary the tickles between two or three tickles. Your baby will begin to anticipate the next tickle, adding to the fun. Tickling nursery rhymes like "Round and Round the Garden" or "This Little Piggy" are also sure to delight your little one.

"GOOD MORNING, BABY!"

Tape-record short greetings from familiar voices, beginning with your own "Good Morning!" when your baby wakes up in the morning, and then adding other familiar voices, such as big sister, little brother, Grandma, a neighbor, or a woof from Bruno the dog. You might also include a few new voices saying the same greetings or even birds tweeting or bells ringing. Play the recording, pausing after each voice to identify the sounds for her.

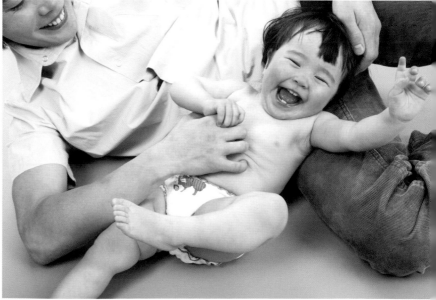

I'M GONNA GET YOU!

Parents have been playing "I'm Gonna Get You!" for generations, and the rules always change as the baby goes from crib to sitting to crawling to toddler to childhood. Grinning and giggling, you make grasping gestures toward Baby in the crib as he laughs and giggles. You cry "I'm gonna get you!" as you reach down, tickle Baby, and then snatch him up for a hug. The next version, when Baby is mobile and you, too, are on hands and knees, entertains both of you as you pretend to pursue a laughing, scuttling Baby across the playroom floor. At the toddler stage, you can introduce your little one to his first tame version of tag, but don't forget to continue to exclaim "I'm gonna get you!" as you chase him. Even at this age the phrase itself will produce squeals of delight.

SIX MONTHS AND UP

PUT YOUR FINGER IN THE AIR

Bath time is quality time for parents and their babies. Most infants look forward to their baths, no matter what time of day. Next bath time, try putting the rubber ducks and plastic sailboats away, and lay your baby facing you. (You can also do this while the baby is on the floor or in her high chair.) Sing the song at right, using the tune of "If You're Happy and You Know It." First follow the song yourself, pointing to the corresponding body parts as you sing. Then take your baby's hand and repeat the song, guiding your baby's fingers to the hair, nose, and toes as indicated in the song. As your baby's coordination develops, add other body parts—knees, elbows, hands, thumbs.

This not only reinforces her awareness of her own body and control of its movements, but it also helps her to later point to her body parts and say their names. As a result, these might become core words for parent–baby messages.

Put Your Finger in the Air

Put your finger in the air
In the air
Put your finger in the air
In the air
Put your finger on your shoe
On your shoe
Put your finger on your shoe
On your shoe
Put your finger on your shoe
And leave it a day or two
Put your finger on your shoe
On your shoe
Put your finger on your tummy
On your tummy
Put your finger on your tummy
On your tummy
Put your finger on your tummy
And think of something yummy
Put your finger on your tummy
On your tummy
Put your fingers all together
All together
Put your fingers all together
All together
Put your fingers all together
And we'll clap for better weather
Put your fingers all together
All together

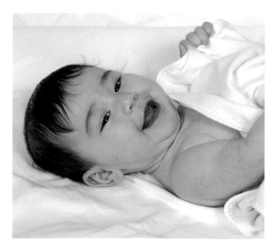

NINE MONTHS AND UP

TALK TO THE HAND!

Make a puppet by drawing eyes, a nose, and a mouth on kitchen oven mitts using permanent felt-tipped markers. Use a favorite outgrown sock of Baby's to create a similar puppet for her. Encourage Baby to talk to her hand. You might use your socks and mitts at the beginning of every snacktime or lunchtime to say hello, offer a treat, and ask for things while practicing "please" and "thank you." This will be a good start for social interaction at the dinner table as Baby grows older and turns the conversation from the hand sock to other family members.

TWELVE MONTHS AND UP

HEAR YE, HEAR YE...!

Have Baby help you decorate a toilet paper tube for her and a paper towel tube for you. Hold one of the tubes to your mouth and say "HELLO EVERYBODY" as if speaking to a crowd on a loudspeaker. You might even move around the room or from room to room to announce an event: "IT'S GRANDMA'S BIRTHDAY TODAY!" "TIME FOR BREAKFAST!" "SALLY DRANK ALL HER ORANGE JUICE." "NAPTIME, NAPTIME!"

Then invite Baby to do the same with her tube, making the announcement to everyone or everything around your home. Once she is able to walk steadily, Baby can follow you around like a loudspeaker on wheels. This game helps your baby learn the difference between talking to one person and talking to the room—or to a crowd. Soon Baby will learn how to talk to her family "audience."

TO SIGN OR NOT TO SIGN?

THE PROS AND CONS OF TEACHING BABY SIGN LANGUAGE

*I*t's frustrating, isn't it? Little Jonathan is frantically gesturing for you to deliver some desired object to him, and you can't for the life of you fathom what he wants. The truck? No. The xylophone? No. The stuffed animal? No, No, NO! Now your little boy is completely frustrated at your lack of comprehension and bursts into an inconsolable wail. Oh, if only he could talk! If only he could just tell you what he wants, how he feels, and what he's thinking! But suppose he could tell you—not with words, but with signs that make his meaning clear. This is not the subtle secret language we've discussed thus far, and that all babies use, but rather a more modern take. This is the controversial topic of baby signing.

Signing for infants has been previously shown to have a positive influence on the development of both hearing-impaired children and those with developmental difficulties. But its more recent incarnation is based on a belief that it can be beneficial for all children.

Over recent years a number of baby-signing books, DVDs, workshops, and courses have found increasing popularity around the world. However, these "prelingual" aids have been greeted with a degree of controversy. On the one hand, proponents of baby signing make great claims for its developmental benefits; on the other, its detractors say it is simply the commercialization of the kind of parent–child gesturing that has been around forever, over which it offers no additional benefits, or worse, that it is detrimental to a child's normal development.

Linda Acredolo, of the University of California at Davis, has been at the forefront of the baby-signing movement since she noticed her daughter Kate sniffing and simultaneously pointing to a rose. Realizing that Kate's sniff was her way of saying "flower," over the next few weeks Acredolo saw her using signs for "more," "hot," and "cat." The little girl, who hadn't yet said her first word, had built a whole vocabulary of signs. This discovery—and the confirmation from other mothers that their children, too, were using signs to communicate—led to an article, coauthored with Susan Goodwyn (a professor of psychology at California State University), entitled "Symbolic Gesturing in Language Development: A Case Study."

In 1996 the pair published their first book, *Baby Signs: How to Talk with Your Baby before Your Baby Can Talk*—which has sold over half a million copies in the United States alone—and followed up its publication

with a round of high-profile publicity on shows such as *Oprah* and *Good Morning America*.

Elsewhere Joseph Garcia had begun to study the use of American Sign Language among hearing babies of hearing parents—work that was to later form the basis of his SIGN with your BABY® program.

Acredolo and Goodwyn's Baby Signs Institute and Garcia's SIGN with your BABY® program are perhaps the two preeminent examples of the baby-signing industry, but there are many others. The claims that are made for baby signing vary from one product or program to the next. However, a review conducted

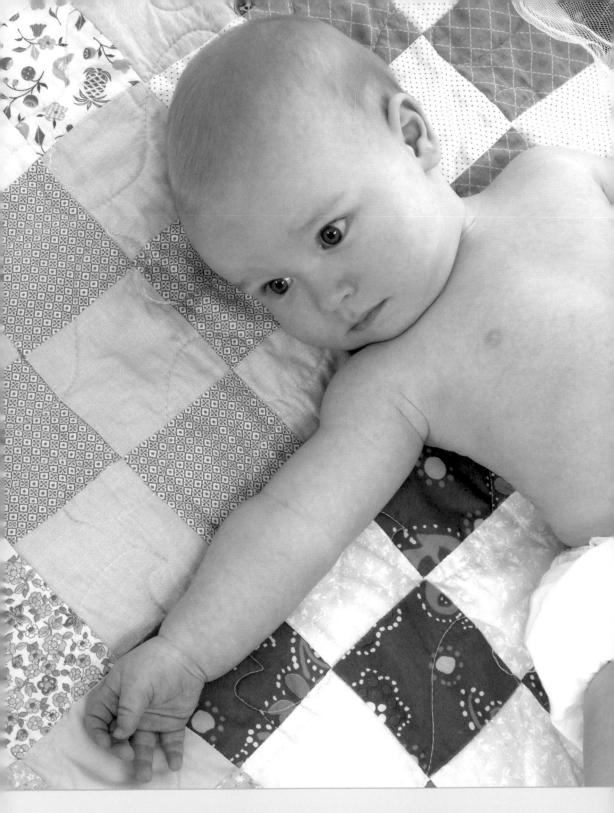

THE HANDS ARE TALKING

Children across cultures spontaneously use their hands to communicate and convey thoughts and ideas. Susan Goldin-Meadow of the University of Chicago established this in a remarkable study of deaf children. Goldin-Meadow profiled ten American children and four Taiwanese children who were profoundly deaf. All were children of hearing parents who had deliberately withheld American Sign Language instruction, planning to have the children instructed in oral speech and lipreading.

Nevertheless the children felt a need to "talk" and so developed their own system of signs and gestures. They had invented signs to signify not only objects and people but also feelings and emotions, like sadness.

By age five they could put strings of signs together and construct whole sentences, even working out their own grammar. They were as skilled at communicating as were their contemporaries who used spoken words.

Like hearing children, deaf children babble— at first, vocally, then using their hands. They even talk to themselves. Goldin-Meadow observed them in their cribs, moving their hands in self-conversation. Although their early words were for objects, people, and places and for actions like hammering or walking, they eventually developed more sophisticated ideas, and could even communicate about acts in the past or expected ones in the future.

by J. Cyne Topshee Johnston and Andrée Durieux-Smith of the University of Ottawa, and Kathleen Bloom of the University of Waterloo found that most claimed similar benefits, such as improved language development, improved parent–child bonding, and a reduction in misbehavior arising from a child's sense of frustration. Certain products also claim to offer lasting benefits for a child's intelligence. Furthermore, signing offers the parent the tantalizing prospect of a window into their child's mind at an age when communication can be unclear to say the least.

At first the rationale for signing seems relatively sound; based on the fact that a child's gross-motor skills develop earlier than his or her fine-motor skills. In other words, a child is able to communicate by signing before he or she has acquired the physical skills to form words with the mouth and tongue. That babies are able to communicate through gesture before they are able to get the same concepts across verbally is undisputed. But that isn't really what the argument is about.

Perhaps the most straightforward criticism of the baby-signing movement is that it simply represents the commercialization of something that parents and children have been doing since time immemorial. Why bother with buying books and DVDs, or paying to go to a workshop or special group, when children are already waving bye-bye or putting their arms in the air to indicate that they want to be picked up?

Many baby-signing programs answer this by saying that not only does the chosen array of signs have a specific rationale, and offer particular benefits, but that learning a formalized system means that confusion is less likely and that this system can be taught to anyone who has contact with your child. Nevertheless, critics, such as Nicola Grove, Ros

BEHIND THE SIGNS

Girls vs. Boys

Girls normally begin to talk several weeks before boys and learn more words sooner. But the two typically learn baby signing at the same pace.

Herman, Gary Morgan, and Bencie Woll (speech and language therapists at the Department of Language and Communication Studies, City University, London) are not put off. Saying, in 2004, that such claims are "disingenuous," and incorrectly suggest that parents are unable to communicate with their child unless they adopt a structured signing system. Going further than this is the concern expressed in a 2003 press release from the Royal College of Speech and Language Therapists, London, that the use of signing should not "take priority over the need for parents to talk to their children."

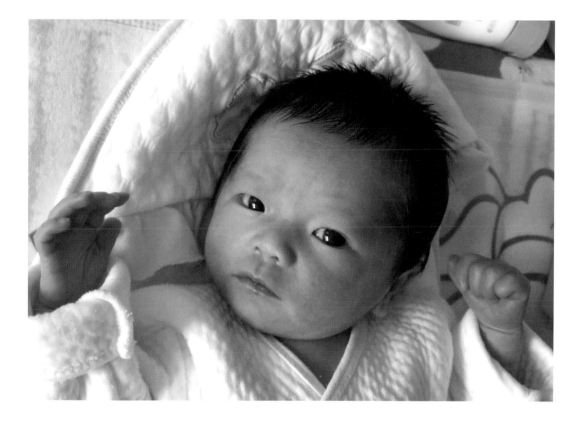

A further criticism is that the evidence of benefits is based on shaky methodology. Certain programs make claims that are solely based on anecdotal evidence, while others cite benefits that have been found in unrelated studies. Moreover, the low number of studies, their typically small sample sizes, and patchy selection and follow-up processes make it very difficult to be confident of their findings. That isn't to say that these findings are incorrect, or that there are no benefits whatsoever, simply that the way in which these studies have been conducted makes it difficult to be convinced that the reported results are not due to other factors.

Baby Fact

It's possible that some of the reported benefits of baby signing arise from increased verbal communication, eye-to-eye contact, and sustained joint attention.

FINDING OUT MORE

If you're interested in teaching your child to sign, but don't know where to start, it's probably worth taking a deeper look at both sides of the argument. To help you on your way, here are a few useful resources.

The book that kick-started the baby-signing movement was Dr. Linda Acredolo and Dr. Susan Goodwyn's *Baby Signs: How to Talk with Your Baby Before Your Baby Can Talk.*

If you're looking for a more skeptical view to counterbalance this, then try the author and journalist Pamela Paul's *Parenting, Inc.*, an investigation of the parenting business and a critique of the commercialization of modern parenthood, which touches upon baby signing.

As mentioned earlier, a great summary of the available evidence, and a good critique of the basis for the claimed benefits of baby signing is "Teaching Gestural Signs to Infants to Advance Child Development: A Review of the Evidence." by J. Cyne Topshee Johnston and Andrée Durieux-Smith of the University of Ottawa, and Kathleen Bloom of the University of Waterloo. It was first published in the journal *First Language*, but the report can now be read on www.research-works.ca/Projects.htm.

Another interesting summary of the debate surrounding the issue is "The Great Baby Signing Debate" by Dr. Gwyneth Doherty-Sneddon, a senior lecturer in psychology at the University of Stirling, Scotland. Originally written for the April 2008 edition of *The Psychologist*, the article can still be read in the online archive at *The Psychologist*'s website (www.thepsychologist.org.uk).

So, what conclusions can we draw? The fairest summing up seems to be that of Topshee Johnston, Durieux-Smith, and Bloom in their 2005 paper, "Teaching Gestural Signs to Infants to Advance Child Development: A Review of the Evidence."

Its authors conclude by saying that "Although one cannot be confident, based on available research evidence, that there are any language, cognitive, or social benefits from the implementation of gestural signing in early infancy, one cannot easily imagine that there are any significant harmful effects."

In short, the jury is out, because there aren't enough high-quality studies in the area. However, it's unlikely that there's a significant downside to baby signing, provided it forms part of the mix of communication with your child, rather than replacing, for example, verbal communication. That said, the evidence provided for its benefits remains unconvincing, and no parent should feel compelled to spend money on the basis of these claims.

LET'S CHAT!

WHY TALKING TO YOUR BABY IS ESSENTIAL TO DEVELOPMENT

"*Good morning, Joel,*" *you say to your ten-day-old son.* "*Aren't you a pretty baby?*" *Then you add,* "*You must be wet, Joel. Let's give you a nice fresh diaper so you're dry.*" *And after the wardrobe change,* "*Now don't you feel better, Joel? Aren't you more comfortable?*"

And then maybe you think, "This is silly. Talking to a tiny baby as if he could understand me. He doesn't understand a word I'm saying."

Well, perhaps he doesn't understand word by word, but Joel senses the rhythm and intonation of your voice. You're not wasting your breath. He's listening. And whether he understands each word or not, it is important—even vital—for his healthy development that you keep up an ongoing conversation with him. Study after study has shown that later intelligence is directly related to how much babies were talked to in the early days of life. Joel points across the room in secret baby language. You respond. The "conversation" pays off.

Psychologists Betty Hart and Todd Risley of the University of Kansas pinpointed these benefits in a three-year study of forty families in Kansas City, Missouri, in 1995. Members of their research team visited each family every month and recorded how much parents talked to their children, what they said, and how they said it. The results were crystal clear. The more parents talked to their kids, the larger the children's vocabularies at three years of age, and the higher their IQ scores. Compared with the children whose parents talked to them infrequently, they were far ahead. A follow-up study when the kids had reached third grade showed they still held this advantage.

BABY TALK 101

Are you one of those people who feels awkward chatting with babies? Or perhaps you're just naturally quiet. Now that you know how important it is to chat with Baby, you understand why it is vital that you overcome your shyness and start up a conversation with Junior, pronto! Here are a few handy tips for tongue-tied parents:

BE YOURSELF: Although some studies have shown that high-pitched "motherese" is beneficial to an infant's cognitive development, speaking to Baby in your normal everyday voice is also beneficial. If baby talk doesn't come naturally to you or makes you feel silly, don't bother with it. Any type of talk with baby is better than none.

THINK PLAY-BY-PLAY: As you feed, bathe, or dress Baby, make a point of describing each step. "Now I'm pulling the socks off your pretty feet. Off come the pants!" Apply this habit to everything you do together.

USE BOOKS TO BREAK THE ICE: Point to the pictures and tell Baby the names of everything you see. The words on the page aren't so important. Even magazines will do the trick.

BE INQUISITIVE: "Did you sleep well?" "Where's Teddy?" "Are you hungry?" Baby won't answer in words, but he might respond with expressions and gestures.

HIRE A CHATTERBOX: If you are planning to hire a caregiver for your infant, favor a chatty candidate over a reserved and quiet one— especially if you are the quiet type yourself.

mostly spoke directly to the child, not simply chattered as they moved around the room. Mom near baby but talking on the telephone to her friends would certainly not achieve the same results.

The parents of the most verbally advanced children began talking to their infants right after birth. It didn't matter much what they said; at first babies were listening to the music more than the words, gaining understanding of how beings "like me" communicated with each other. Positive messages had more impact than negative ones. "Oh, that's

But it wasn't just quantity of words that counted. It was the number of words directly addressed to the child or spoken in response to the child's gestures or actions. The children who benefited most had parents who regularly picked up on a bit of the preverbal child's body language and commented on it. "Yes, Joel, that's your *teddy bear*! Your *teddy bear* is right over there! Do you want me to bring you your *teddy bear*?" "Did you like your *juice*, Joel? Would you like more *juice*?" And it made a difference how often the parents called the child by name and repeated the name.

Hart and Risley also found, perhaps not surprisingly, that the more variety parents used in their speech, the more children learned. Those children did best whose parents peppered their conversation with nouns, verbs, and adjectives. They did not rely on basic baby talk, but rather spoke in full sentences, used descriptions, and drew word pictures. They

great, Joel! You drank all your juice!" Interestingly, in some of the low-scoring families, the researchers said the most commonly heard phrases were "No!" and "Don't do that!"

Repetition is also important—in fact, it is the key to success in language development, one researcher has said. When you follow Joel's extended finger and focused gaze to his target, you say, "Yes! The *fire truck*! That's your *fire truck*! You want the *fire truck*, Joel!" repeating, stressing, and clearly pronouncing the word to help insert it into his structure of understood language. Likewise, when he wordlessly points, you point too, demonstrating that

Baby Fact:

Babies who are talked to a great deal are very vocal. Babies who are normally cared for in silence vocalize much less.

the gesturing finger and the secret language is one real way that people tell others their wants and ideas. The practice of "mirroring," which is part of the same lesson in repetition, provides the child with an action or facial expression that directly reflects his own and tells him his message is being received. Making your face look like Baby's face tells him who he is, what he does, and even how he feels—your responsive smile reinforces the smile on Baby's face.

Your tone of voice carries messages, too. One researcher demonstrated that if you smile at a baby but speak in a gruff voice, Baby will become upset, whereas if you frown yet speak in a soothing voice, Baby is calmed all the same.

Words and gestures work together to foster communication between you and your infant. The secret language of babies—"spoken" in body movements, facial expressions, and pointing fingers—is Baby's side of the equation. This is his means of reaching out to you, and "speaking" to you. Your side of the equation is the spoken, reassuring words he needs to hear from you.

And above all, listen. Not just with your ears— because you now know that your baby speaks to you in many silent ways—but with your eyes, senses, natural instincts, and with an open heart and mind. Listen and hear all that Baby has to say, and you will begin to forge a bond of communication that will hopefully last well into his adulthood.

THE LAST WORD

AND THE FIRST

The secret language of babies is an important step in your child's development, but it is only a stepping stone to meaningful adult speech. By about a year of age—a bit later for boys, a bit earlier for girls—the first recognizable spoken word pops out of Baby's mouth. Possibly, for a few days before this milestone, he has been making intentional vocalizations that his parents did not recognize as words. Nevertheless, that initial "Mama" or "Dada" is the beginning of true adult communication.

A year later, at age two, a child can usually utter about fifty words; these mostly identify familiar people or objects like "Mama" or "cookie." Furthermore, at this stage, Baby can usually put two words together in a simple, understandable sentence, such as: "Lost cookie." From then on, he will understand many more and move forward to a larger, richer vocabulary.

The accompanying chart by the American Speech and Hearing Associations skims the course of communication development from infant gestures and "secret language" to eight-year-old speech. Of course, not all children follow this track precisely—some are more talkative than others, some are more precocious than others, and some are shy and tend to keep their thoughts to themselves. What's more, communicative growth does not necessarily progress at a steady rate; the pattern may be uneven or occur in sudden spurts. Despite a newfound ability to speak, your toddler won't totally let go of his "secret language" for many years yet. Some vestiges of it—such as pointing—will indeed persist into adulthood.

LANGUAGE DEVELOPMENT CHART

How Does Your Child Hear And Talk?

AGE	HEARING, UNDERSTANDING, AND TALKING
Birth to three months	Startles to loud sounds. Quiets or smiles when spoken to. Seems to recognize your voice and quiets if crying. Increases or decreases sucking behavior in response to sound. Makes pleasure sounds (cooing, gooing). Cries differently for different needs. Smiles when sees you.
Four to six months	Moves eyes in direction of sounds. Responds to changes in tone of your voice. Notices toys that make sounds. Pays attention to music. Babbling in a speech–like way with many different sounds, including *p, b, m*. Vocalizes excitement and displeasure. Makes gurgling sounds when left alone and when playing with you.
Seven months to one year	Enjoys games like peekaboo and pat-a-cake. Turns and looks in direction of sounds. Listens when spoken to. Recognizes words for common items like "cup," "shoe," "juice." Begins to respond to requests and commands ("Come here!" " Want more?"). Babbling has both long and short groups of sounds, such as "tata upup bibibibi." Uses speech or non-crying sounds to get and keep attention. Imitates different speech sounds. Has one or two words (bye-bye, dada, mama) although they may not be clear.

LANGUAGE DEVELOPMENT CHART

How Does Your Child Hear And Talk?

AGE	HEARING, UNDERSTANDING AND TALKING
One to two years	Points to a few body parts when asked. Follows simple commands and understands simple questions ("Roll the ball," "Where's your shoe?"). Listens to simple stories, songs, and rhymes. Points to pictures in a book when named. Says more words every month. Uses some one- or two-word questions ("Where Kitty?" "Go bye bye?"). Puts two words together ("more cookie," "mommy book"). Uses many different consonant sounds at the beginning of words.
Two to three years	Understands differences in meaning ("go–stop," "in–on," "big–little," "up–down"). Follows two simultaneous requests ("Get the book and put it on the table."). Has a word for almost everything. Uses two or three-word "sentences" to talk about and ask for things. Speech is understood by familiar listeners most of the time. Often asks for or directs attention to objects by naming them.
Three to four years	Hears you when you call from another room. Hears television or radio at the same loudness level as other family members. Understands simple questions: Who? What? Where? Why? Talks about activities at school or at friends' homes. People outside the family usually understand child's speech. Uses a lot of sentences that have four or more words. Usually talks easily without repeating syllables or words.

LANGUAGE DEVELOPMENT CHART

How Does Your Child Hear And Talk?

AGE	HEARING, UNDERSTANDING AND TALKING
Four to five years	Pays attention to a short story and answers simple questions about it. Hears and understands most of what is said at home and in school. Voice sounds clear like other children's. Uses sentences that give lots of detail (for example, " I like to read my books"). Tells stories that stick to topic. Communicates easily with other children and adults. Says most sounds correctly except a few like *l, s, r, v, z, ch, sh, th*. Uses the same grammar as the rest of the family.

Chart courtesy of the American Speech and Hearing Association

ABOUT THE AUTHORS

*S*ally Valente Kiester and Edwin Kiester Jr. were a husband-wife team whose writings on health, science, education, and child development have been widely published in the United States and around the world. They coauthored the Better Homes & Gardens New Baby Book *and* Eating Healthy, *a* Better Homes & Gardens *guide to better nutrition. They have co-written numerous articles on education and health for* Reader's Digest *and its international editions.* The Secret Language of Babies *is their twelfth book.*

Sally Valente Kiester held a doctorate in education from Stanford University. In addition to her publications in professional journals, she was a consultant in continuing education and professional development. She served on the board of the Palo Alto Foundation for Education and held a leadership position in the American Association of University Women, which named her Outstanding Woman of the Year 2005 for the state of Pennsylvania.

Edwin Kiester Jr. has been a top editor on several national magazines, a staff writer for *Reader's* *Digest*, and a regular contributor to *Smithsonian Magazine*. He has written more than two thousand articles for major publications. He has also edited the *Better Homes & Gardens Family Medical Guide*. He has been named an honorary member of Sigma Xi, the international scientific research society, for his writing about the sciences and health. The Kiesters made their home in England, Spain, Mexico, the Philippines, Hong Kong, New York, and California. Edwin Keister Jr. now lives in Pittsburgh, Pennsylvania.

ACKNOWLEDGMENTS

This book has had a long period of germination and, therefore, has a long roster of persons who deserve thanks for their contributions, support, and willingness to tolerate repeated phone calls, e-mails, and requests for publications, scientific papers, and guidance.

The book's genesis dates back to our first edition of the *Better Homes & Gardens New Baby Book* and to later articles on child development for *Smithsonian, Reader's Digest*, and other publications. Gerry Knox, then of *Better Homes & Gardens*, and Norman Smith, then of *Reader's Digest*, thus deserve special, if belated, thanks.

The husband–wife team of Patricia Kuhl and Andrew Meltzoff of the University of Washington, internationally known for their pioneering child-development insights, were never too busy to carry on long conversations about their work, to set us straight at times of confusion, and in Pat's case to demonstrate vividly the experiments in preverbal communication that have brought her renown. Andy's explanation of his "like me" theory as the underpinning of child–parent relationships gave shape to the final manuscript.

Colwyn Trevarthen of the University of Edinburgh in Scotland welcomed our transatlantic inquiries and provided many references from his weighty works.

Roberta Minchnick Golinkoff of the University of Delaware and Kathy Hirsh-Pasek of Temple University sat still for enlightening visits to their labs and for long telephone interviews, meanwhile sharing reminiscences of our mutual *alma mater*, the University of Pittsburgh. Susan Goldin-Meadow of the University of Chicago endured many late-night phone conversations about her work with deaf children and how they develop their own communicative methods without words. Paul Holinger, M.D., willingly shared his findings about babies' facial expressions and the messages they convey. Barry Lester of Brown University guided us through the ways infants use crying to convey all sorts of messages. Lise Eliot, of the Chicago Medical School, herself the mother of young children, took time out to describe the physical and neurological changes that enable babies to create their secret language. And, finally, Linda Acredolo engagingly explained to us how her own child's made-up sign language led to the exciting "Baby Signs" movement that is spreading worldwide.

We thank Hannah and Natalie Soler for giving us the impetus to write this book, and to their parents, Maria Teresa and Joe Soler.

The Breitwiesers—Jochen, Katja, Nick, and especially Lucy, fluent in two languages at the age of three and our German-English interpreter—were an early inspiration and gave us a European perspective. They also taught us to sing "Hoppe, Hoppe Reiter," the German version of the classic knee-bouncing song used with children across cultures.

Another inspiration was Marge Collins of Palo Alto, California, a gifted reading teacher with many insights into how children move from preverbal communication to spoken words, to the magic of print. An old college classmate and proud father, Richard Ferketic, led us to his daughter, Michele Ferketic Eberhard of the American Hearing and Speech Association, who in turn opened many doors to experts in communicative development. We also thank Evelyn Murrin for leading us to work in early child development sponsored by Peace Links of Pittsburgh.

Even in the Internet age, libraries are indispensable to inquisitive authors. We thank the staffs of the Carnegie Library of Pittsburgh and the Hillman Library of the University of Pittsburgh.

Sally Valente Kiester, Ed.D.
Edwin Kiester Jr.

BIBLIOGRAPHY

Acredolo, Linda, and Susan Goldwyn, with Doug Abrams. *Baby Signs*. Chicago: Contemporary Books, 2002.

Blasi, Wendy S., and Roni Cohen Lieberman, general editors, *Baby Play*. San Francisco: Creative Publishing International, 2004.

Bloom, Lois, *One Word at a Time*. The Hague: Mouton, 1973.

Bloom, Lois, *Breaking the Language Barrier.* Commentary by Kathy Hirsh-Pasek and George C. Hollisch, Roberta Golinkoff. Boston, Blackwell Publishers, 2000.

Bloom, Lois, *The Transition from Infancy to Language.* Cambridge, U.K., and New York, 1993.

Bloom, Lois, and Erin Tanker. *The Intentional Model and Language Acquisition.* Boston: Blackwell Publishers, 2001.

Bloom, Lois and Margaret Lahey, *Language Development and Language Disorders.* New York: Wiley, 1978.

Brazelton, Berry, *Infants and Mothers: Differences in Development.* New York: Dell Publishing, 1983.

Carpenter, Malina, Katherine Nagell and Michael Tomasello, with commentary by George Butterworth. *Social Cognition, Joint Attention and Communicative Competence from 9 to 15 Months of Age.* Chicago: University of Chicago Press, 1998.

Eisenberg, Arlene, Murkoff, Heidi E., and Hathaway, Sandee E., *What to Expect the First Year.* New York: Workman Publishing, 1989.

Eliot, Lise. *What's Going On In There?* How the Brain and Mind Develop in the First Five Years of Life. New York: Bantam Books, 1999.

Goldin-Meadow, Susan: *Hearing Gesture: How Our Hands Help Us Think.* Cambridge, Massachusetts, Belknap Press of Harvard University Press, 2003.

Goldin-Meadow, Susan, *The Resilience of Language.* New York: Psychology Press, 2003.

Goldin-Meadow, Susan, and Carolyn Myland. *Gestural Communication in Deaf Children.* Chicago: University of Chicago Press for the Society for Research in Child Development, 1984.

Golinkoff, Roberta M., and Kathy Hirsh-Pasek, *How Babies Talk: The Magic and Mystery of Language in the First Three Years of Life.* New York: Dutton, 1999.

Gopnik, Alison and Andrew N. Meltzoff and Patricia K. Kuhl, *The Scientist in the Crib.* New York: William Morrow, 1999.

Gruber, Howard E., and J. Jacques Voneche, *The Essential Piaget.* New York: Basic Books, 1977.

Hirsh-Pasek, Kathy, and Roberta M. Golinkoff, *Einstein Didn't Use Flash Cards.* Emmaus, Pennsylvania: Rodale Press, 2003.

Holinger, Paul C., *What Babies Say Before They Can Talk.* New York: Fireside, 2003.

Jaffe, Joseph, *The Rhythm of Dialogue in Infancy.* With commentary by Philippe Rochat and Daniel N. Stern. Boston: Blackwell Publishers, 2001.

Kiester, Edwin Jr., and Sally Valente Kiester, *Better Homes & Gardens New Baby Book.* Des Moines, Iowa: Meredith, 1976, 1988, and 1992.

Leach, Penelope, *Your Baby and Child: From Birth to Age Five, New Edition.* New York: Alfred A. Knopf, 1995.

Lester, Barry M., ed., and C.F. Zachariah Boykdois. *Infant Crying.* New York: Plenum Press, 1985.

Lester, Barry M., with Catherine O'Neill Grace. *Why Is My Baby Crying?* New York: HarperCollins, 2005.

Marshall, Connie, *From Here to Maternity.* Minden, Nevada: Conmar Publishing, 1997.

Meltzoff, Andrew N., and Wolfgang Prinz, eds., *The Imitative Mind.* Cambridge, U.K., and New York: Cambridge University Press, 2002.

Nadel, Jacqueline, *Imitation in Infancy.* Cambridge, U.K., and New York: Cambridge University Press, 1999.

Rochat, Philippe, *The Infant's World.* Cambridge, Massachusetts: Cambridge University Press, 2004.

Rochat, Philippe, ed., *Early Social Cognition.* Mahwah, New Jersey: L. Erlbaum Associates, C 1999.

Sanger, Sirgay, *Baby Talk, Parent Talk.* New York: Doubleday, 1991.

Shelov, Steven P., ed., *The American Academy of Pediatrics: Caring for Your Baby and Young Child: Birth to Age Five, Revised Edition.* New York: Bantam Books, 1998.

Starting Young℠: *Supporting Parents for Peaceful Lifestyles.* A Peace Links publication. Brackenridge, Pennsylvania: Motinicua Press, 2005.

Stern, Daniel N., *The Diary of a Baby.* New York: Basic Books, 1990.

Stern, Daniel N., *The First Relationship: Mother and Infant.* Cambridge, Massachusetts: Harvard University Press, 1977.

Stern, Daniel N., *The Interpersonal World of the Infant.* New York: Basic Books, 1985.

Stern, Daniel N., *The Motherhood Constellation.* New York: Basic Books, 1995.

ARTICLES

Acredolo, L. and S. Goodwyn, "Sign Language Among Hearing Infants: The Spontaneous Development of Symbolic Gestures." *From Gesture to Language in Hearing and Deaf Children,* V. Volterra and C. Erting, eds. New York: Springger-Verlag, 1990.

Acredolo, L. and S. Goodwyn, "Symbolic Gesturing in Normal Infants." *Child Development* 59: 450-466.

Andruski, J. and P.K. Kuhl. "The Acoustic Structure of Vowels in Mothers' Speech to Infants and Adults." *The Proceedings of the 1996 International Conference on Spoken Language Processing,* vol. 3, pp. 1545-1548, 1996.

Brooks, R. and A.N. Meltzoff. "The Development of Gaze Following and its Relation to Language." *Developmental Science,* 2005.

Damasio, A.R. and H. Damasio. "Brain and Language." *Scientific American* 267: 88-95, 1992.

D'Arcangelo, M. "The Scientist in the Crib: A Conversation with Andrew Meltzoff." In *The Science of Learning,* v. 58, no. 3, November 2000, 8-13, 2000.

Golinkoff, R.M. "'I Beg Your Pardon?' The Preverbal Negotiation of Failed Messages." *Journal of Child Language,* 13, (1986.) 455-476, 1985.

Golinkoff, R.M. "When is Communication a 'Meeting of Minds'?" *Journal of Child Language* 20 (1993), 199-207, 1991.

Gopnik, A. "The Acquisition of 'Gone!' and the Development of the Object Concept." *Journal of Child Language* 11: 273-92, 1984.

Gopnik, A. "Conceptual and Semantic Development as Theory Change: The Case of Object Permanence." *Mind and Language* 3: 197-216, 1988.

Grieser, D.L. and P.K.Kuhl. "Acoustic Determinants of Infant Preference for Motherese Speech." *Infant Behavior and Development* 10: 279-93, 1987.

Harding, C.G. and R.M. Golinkoff. "The Origins of Intentional Vocalizations in Prelinguistic Infants." *Child Development*, 1979, 33-40, 1979.

Hart, B. and T.R. Risley. "American Parenting of Language-Learning Children: Persisting Differences in Family-Child Interactions Observed in Natural Home Environments," *Developmental Psychology* 28, 1096-1105, 1992.

Joseph, R. "Cingulate Gyrus." *Neuropsychiatry, Neuropsychology, Clinical Neuroscience,* Third edition. New York: Academic Press, 2000.

Kiester, Edwin Jr. "Accents Are Forever," *Smithsonian*, January 2001.

Kuhl, P.K. "Learning and Representation in Speech and Language," *Current Opinion in Neurobiology*, 4:812-822, 1994.

Kuhl, P.K. "Innate Predispositions and the Effects of Experience in Speech Perception: The Native Language Magnet Theory." B. de Boysson-Bardies, S. de Schonen, P. Jusczyk, P. McNeilage & J. Mortons (eds.), *Developmental Neurocognition:*

Speech and Face Processing in the First Year of Life. Boston: Kluwer, 1993.

Kuhl, P.K., K.A. Williams, F. Lacerda, K.N. Stevens and B. Lindblom. "Linguistic Experience Alters Phonetic Perception in Infants by 6 Months of Age." *Science* 255:606-608, 1992.

Liszkowski, U. and M. Carpenter, A. Henning, T. Striano & M. Tomasello, 2004. "Twelve-Month-Olds Point to Share Attention and Interest." *Developmental Science*, 7, 297-307, 2001.

Meltzoff, A.N., "Imitation and Other Minds: The 'Like Me Hypothesis.'" *Perspective on Imitation: From Neuroscience to Social Science*, S. Hurley & N. Chater, eds. vol. 2, pp.55-77. Cambridge, Massachusetts: MIT Press, 2005.

Meltzoff, A. and M. Keith Moore. "Imitation of Facial and Manual Gestures by Human Neonates." *Science,* New Series, v. 198: 4312, 75-78, 1977.

Trevarthen, C. and K.J. Aitken. "Infant Intersubjectivity: Research, Theory and Clinical Applications." *Annual Research Review, Journal of Child Psychology and Psychiatry*, 42 (1), 3-48, 2001.

Trevarthen, C. "Communication and Cooperation in Early Infancy: A Description of Primary Intersubjectivity." *Before Speech*, M. Bullowa, ed. 321-47. New York: Cambridge University Press, 1979.

Trevarthen, C. and P. Hubley. "Secondary Intersubjectivity: Confidence, Confiding and Acts of Meaning in the First Year." *Action, Gesture and Symbol: The Emergence of Language*, ed. A. Lock, 183-229. New York: Academic Press, 1978.

INDEX